PRAISE FOR *THE ACTIVIST*

"*The Activist* by Daniel Fried is one of those rare creative works that combine meticulous scholarly research with literary sensibilities and concerns about the world we are living in. The book brings the ancient Chinese Daoist ideas to bear on issues of social activism in contemporary America in a surprisingly intriguing and relevant form and makes very enjoyable reading."
   —**Zhang Longxi, author of *A History of Chinese Literature* and *World Literature as Discovery***

"Daniel Fried is an accomplished scholar of Daoism. This philosophy has usually been associated in the popular mind with mysticism. Fried, however, provides us with unique insights into the social and political relevance of this philosophical school of thought for our times."
   —**Kim-Chong Chong, Professor Emeritus, Hong Kong University of Science and Technology and author of *Zhuangzi's Critique of the Confucians***

"*The Activist* is one of the most lyrical works of English nonfiction I have ever read. You can feel the yin and yang of Chinese literature inside it, like the noonday sun and the midnight moon shining at the same time."
   —**Joyce Zhang, Chinese translator of Alice Munro's *Dance of the Happy Shades* and *Too Much Happiness***

"Capturing many of the insights of classical Daoism, Professor Daniel Fried's insightful book brings out the strategic usefulness of making change slowly and gently in politics and governance in the modern world."
   —**Laifong Leung, Professor Emerita, University of Alberta and author of *Contemporary Chinese Fiction Writers***

"A powerful inspiration for Chinese or other minority writers. *The Activist* encourages confronting racism not through direct conflict but with clarity and inner strength. Rooted in Daoist wisdom, it offers a path of resistance and reconciliation, guiding writers to turn storytelling into a quiet yet deeply transformative act of protest."
— **Cathy Shi, president, Edmonton Chinese Writing Club and anti-racism activist**

"I've read countless books on protest, but none have done what Daniel Fried's *The Activist* does. It doesn't cheerlead, doesn't lecture, doesn't dress up old tactics in new slogans. Instead, it slips under the surface of what activism is usually believed to mean and pulls something ancient, unfamiliar, and quietly subversive into view. This is a book for people who have grown tired of shouting, who sense that sometimes the most radical act is not to fight harder but to move differently. It draws from Daoism not to exoticize but to excavate a philosophy that has always known how to work with the grain of power rather than crash against it. What emerges is not just a strategy but a way of seeing. What gives authority to this way of seeing is the author himself, a rare kind of Daoist thinker who, as I know, embodies the integration of knowing and doing, living Daoism instead of just interpreting it. Fried's new book won't stir your anger. It might, though, change your instincts."
— **Dr. Hongbing Yu, former president of the Semiotic Society of America and associate professor at Toronto Metropolitan University**

"Using contemporary and historical examples of protest movements, Fried has painstakingly analyzed and revealed how collective actions meant for effecting positive social changes are often hijacked and derailed by twisted words, rules, and boundaries. The author delicately nudges the reader to be en garde of the meaning of words said, actions taken, and their alignment with the cause and demanded outcome in collective actions."

—**Steve C. F. Au-Yeung, director of Daoist Studies, Po Yuen Taoist Centre Society, Vancouver**

"Some books are compelling because readers can't put them down. Fried's *The Activist* is compelling because readers will need to put it down and sit in quiet with it, adopting the Daoist non-action (wu wei) the book advances to find their way to its new but very old and very unexpected ideas about changing the world and having a future for everyone."

—**Dr. Jennifer Quist, award-winning author of** *The Apocalypse of Morgan Turner, Sistering,* **and** *Love Letters of the Angels of Death*

"In an era when others jump at the chance to twist our words and misconstrue our actions, how we handle such situations has become critically important. When both quiet and vocal resistance are met with forceful pushback, what are we to do? Is there not a middle path, one that can yield results without antagonizing others? In *The Activist*, Daniel Fried passionately and convincingly argues Yes! Recasting the teachings of ancient Chinese Daoism for the modern, conflict-prone reader, Fried shares how reading, teaching, and applying Daoism to his own life has resulted in a more joyful and humorous outlook. This is a book for our times, in response to our times. It will cause you to think, laugh, and shake your head in amazement, but most important, it will stir you into action!"

—**David Chai, associate professor at The Chinese University of Hong Kong**

"*The Activist* challenged (like all good art does) my perception of modern-day social activism. By drawing on historical protests and ancient Chinese Daoism theory in a very accessible and educational way, Fried invites us to reflect on how we can strategically impact the issues we care about in our ever-changing world."
  —Jordon Hon, visual artist and community organizer

THE ACTIVIST
A Daoist Protest Manual

DANIEL FRIED

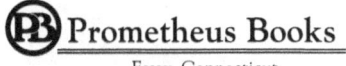
Prometheus Books

Essex, Connecticut

Prometheus Books

An imprint of The Globe Pequot Publishing Group, Inc.
64 South Main St.
Essex, CT 06426
www.GlobePequot.com

Copyright © 2026 by Daniel Fried

All rights reserved. No part of this book may be reproduced in any form or by any electronic or mechanical means, including information storage and retrieval systems, without written permission from the publisher, except by a reviewer who may quote passages in a review.

British Library Cataloguing in Publication Information available

Library of Congress Cataloging-in-Publication Data Available

ISBN 978-1-4930-9138-6 (paperback)
ISBN 978-1-4930-9139-3 (ebook)

Contents

Spelling and Pronunciation Guide. viii
Preface. xii
Introduction: What Is This Book? 1
Activism Dao's and Daon'ts 19
How to Fight Fascism Lying Down 23
The Activist 62
    Saying. 63
    Acting. 71
    Resting 79
    Nothing. 87
    Aiming 95
    Strategizing 104
    Leading 113
Master of the Encampment 121
A Quick History Lesson: Daoism and Chinese Social Movements 176
Further Reading on Daoism and Chinese History. . . 192
Acknowledgments 195

Spelling and Pronunciation Guide

Throughout this book, the now-standard pinyin system is used for all Chinese names and titles, which indicates pronunciations in modern Mandarin (the standard dialect of all public governance, commerce, and media). Unfortunately, the actual sounds indicated by pinyin are not intuitive for native speakers of English; in addition, many readers will still be familiar with the older Wade-Giles system of transliteration. Here is a quick guide to writing and pronouncing several names used in this book with the closest equivalents to normal English phonemes; full pinyin pronunciation guides can be found online.

Beijing (the same place as "Peking"): The "j" is hard, as in "jewel," not pronounced like the "zhuzh" sound in words like "Asia."

Cao Cao (Wade-Giles: "Ts'ao-Ts'ao") The "C" is a "ts" sound; "ao" rhymes with "cow."

Changbai: "Chang" rhymes with "long"; "bai" is pronounced as "bye."

Chu: as in "Jimmy Choo."

dao (Wade-Giles: "Tao"): is pronounced as the "dow" in "endowment."

Daodejing (Wade-Giles: "Tao Te Ching"): "de" is pronounced as "undeserving"; "jing" is as in "jingle."

Deng Xiaoping: "Deng" is pronounced "dung." "X" is pronounced as "sh," "iao" like the comic-book exclamation "Yow!" Hence, "Dung Sh-yow-ping."

Han Fei: "Han" is as in "Han Solo"; "Fei" is "fay."

Hanfeizi: as above, but with a "dz" ending.

Hu Yaobang: "Hu" is as "Who." "Yao" rhymes with "vow," "bang" with "strong."

Laozi (Wade-Giles: "Lao Tzu"): "Lao" is pronounced as the second syllable in "allow"; "zi" is pronounced as "dz."

Liezi (Wade-Giles: "Lieh-tzu"): "Lie" is pronounced as if "l" + "y" + a short "e" sound as in "wet"; "zi" sounds like "dz."

Li Peng: "Li" is as "Lee"; "Peng" rhymes with "wrung."

Miluo: "Mi" is like the English "me." "Luo" is tricky: "l" is just "l," but "u" is "w," and "o" sounds like "aw" when pronounced by someone with a New Jersey accent. Overall, then: "mee-lwaw."

Mo Di (Wade-Giles: "Mo Ti"): "Mo" is somewhat close to "maw," and "Di" is simply "dee."

neijuan: "nei" sounds like a "nay" vote; "j" is just "j," "u" is a "w" sound, and "an" here rhymes with "zen," so as a whole *neijuan* sounds like "nay-jwen."

Nü Wa: "Nü" is best approximated by English "new"; "Wa" rhymes with "ah."

Qin (Wade-Giles: "Tsin"): "Q" has a ch-sound, so: "chin."

Shun: There's an invisible "w" sound here, so: "Shwun."

Sichuan (Wade-Giles: "Ssu-ch'uan"): "Si" is very hard to produce using English sounds, but a reasonable approximation is the "si" in "silk"; the sounds in "chuan" are "ch" + "w" + "on."

Sima Qian: (Wade-Giles: "Ssu-Ma Ch'ien"): "Si" is as above, "ma" is "ma," "Q" has a ch-sound, and "ian" is close to "yen." So: "Si-ma Ch-yen."

Sunzi (Wade-Giles: "Sun Tzu"): "Sun" is pronounced like the English word "swoon" would be if the double-o sound were the same as it is in "good"; "zi" is the "dz" sound.

tangping: "Tang" is pronounced like the English word "tong"; "ping" rhymes with "sling."

Tiananmen: "Tian" rhymes with "yen," "an" is pronounced "on," and "men" rhymes with "done."

Wei: same as "way."

Xu: "X" is like "sh"; hence, "shoo" and not "zoo."

Yijing (Wade-Giles: "I Ching"): "yi" rhymes with "tea"; "jing" rhymes with "ring."

yin-yang (Wade-Giles: "yin-yang"): "yin" rhymes with "in"; "yang" rhymes with "long."

Yu: the pronoun "you" is the closest English comes to this name; the sound is closer to the French "u," as in "tu."

Zhao Ziyang: "Zh" is close to "j," "ao" is as "brow," "Zi" like the "dz" sound in "kids," and "yang" like "throng." Hence, "J-ow Dz-yong."

Spelling and Pronunciation Guide

Zhuangzi or *Zhuang Zhou* (Wade-Giles: "Chuang Tzu"): "Zhu" is pronounced as the English letters "j" and "w"; "uang" is pronounced as "ong" (as in "bong"). "Zhou" is pronounced as the English names "Joe" or "Jo."

Preface

This is a book for people who want to do good in the world.

It is not a book for people who want to be seen to do good in the world.

Sometimes, doing the very most you can do to make the world a better place will feel like doing too little. Sometimes, doing nothing at all is the very most you can do, because any action will only make things worse. It is always better to do little or nothing—and stay invisible—than to make things worse—and look heroic.

Today we are beset by an epidemic of heroically making things worse. This is caused by a number of things: genuinely heroic historical models that don't apply, the unquestioned assumptions of late liberal democracies, pathologies of performing for virality, and the ideological autophagies of Ourobouros movements on the left and the right. Perhaps social scientist specialists can tease out the patterns of cause. The effects are apparent everywhere: the people who say they care the most about making the world a better place are the same ones who are spreading hatred and trauma most quickly.

Most of what I know about making the world a better place I have learned from Chinese people. Some of that has been from China's ancient philosophers. Just as much has been from Chinese colleagues, friends, and relatives who are not philosophers but who have mastered the simple and powerful skill of seeing the world clearly and understanding the scope of one's own action. They have modeled for me how to do the most good by finding doors that are already half-open and pushing gently on them.

I hope that those who read this book, both protestors and non-protestors, can learn the power of softness. Though this book is my own writing, that softness isn't mine to claim authorship over: I am just a transmitter, not a creator. At the same time, the power to be an agent of peace belongs to anyone willing to assimilate themselves to the form of that power.

It's a long road for most of us to learn how to be that kind of person. As someone said, though, a journey of a thousand miles begins underfoot.

Introduction: What Is This Book?

1

This book is about action in the world. Which actions work? Which actions don't? How do we save, and how do we harm?

We fetishize the fury of motion—a blur becomes our totem. The goal is ultimately expendable, so long as we are doing something. Rise up. Strike back. Lean in. Fight on. Speak out. Hands off. Our clichés testify against us: we demand motion and direction, not effects. Taking a bold stand in opposition to injustice is celebrated, even if the bold stand is useless or counterproductive. Remaining passive, pliant, or submissive in the face of injustice is contemptible—no one considers the pliancy that ensnares. Acting quickly and quietly in carefully calibrated ways never receives acclaim or approbation because it is never noticed, even when it tips death back over into life.

The confusion of appearance for reality is easy to see and to mock in others. Check your social media feeds: how many on the left mock Trump's fans for thinking that the gold-plated huckster-ism betokens true savvy, or that the all-caps trollery signifies true steel? Every correct-thinking reader of solid political and business journalism understands that tough-guy tariffs on China are a way of mugging for the cameras, not an economic masterstroke. And then the same reader cheers on the thoroughly grandiose and spectacular nationwide protest demanding Trump's immediate resignation that will, with complete cosmic certainty, not result in his resignation. We seem addicted to the phantasmic satisfactions of pure image, even at the cost of the real and gritty substance of the just.

Some problems don't have a solution. Some solutions are slow and boring. Learning to win the best available solution requires breaking addictions to destructive structures of thought.

Daoism is methadone for these addictions. It's still a kinda sorta structure of its own, and it would be better to just be spontaneously and perfectly enlightened to the complete reality of time and space. But at least Daoism can start to break up the harm of being all in on the routinized schemata through which most people process the world.

That's why, when this book explains how we can save, and how we can harm, it starts from Daoism.

2

Daoism is a weird philosophy to put forward as a foundation for social action.

It's hard to know if it is a philosophy at all. The earliest Daoist texts are usually opposed to the kind of logical argumentation from first principles that philosophy is supposed to be. A few centuries after those texts, it evolved into a full religion, with pantheons of gods, church structures, ethical codes, and worship practices. In the hands of elite literati, Daoism often became more a catalog of aesthetic and stylistic gestures than a set of distinct claims.

When Daoism is most philosophical, it skids away from social engagement. One of its core principles is *wuwei*, conventionally translated as "nonaction." It praises aloofness. Its heroes and saints are weird loners who hang out in caves.

Daoists often self-exile to the margins of Chinese society—but margins are a powerful space. Margins define the society they critique. Margins are the staging area for revolutions.

The "nonaction" that lies at the heart of Daoism is not a complete absence of doing. It is a soft doing, a way of moving through the interstices of the world so that one's actions never meet with resistance. Sometimes that means sitting alone in a cave, but sometimes it means making the tiniest slice at the jointures of the world that brings down structures in a heap.

3

The origin of this book was in the pro-Palestinian protests that roiled campuses during the 2023–2024 school year. As the chair of a university department, I had a perfect viewpoint from which to watch spectacular anger and confrontation play itself out on my campus. As a scholar of classical Chinese literature and philosophy with a particular focus on Daoism, I could see with clarity why the protests were fated to end in chaos and pain without shortening the war. By choosing proximate targets over useful targets, tactics over strategy, and confrontation over engagement, that movement worked hard to achieve exactly what it achieved: backlash. Watching those campus disasters play out over the course of a slow school year determined me to write what I knew.

As I have been writing, a historical tragedy larger than campus politics has progressed. The reelection of Trump has accelerated the decline and fall of American democracy. Once again, there are calls for more of the same. Resistance. Protest marches. Speeches. Slogans. General strikes. This past April, the Hands Off! protests drew three million people across the United States. Three million people may feel that they have taken a stand, but Trump has not taken his hands off anything yet. (Spoiler alert: he never will.)

That kind of massive, coordinated street protest can be effective in achieving national change in very specific and unusual circumstances. Most of the time, it is useless. But marching around and chanting is a good, solid-feeling physical carrier of hope for change—just like a lottery ticket is a good physical carrier of hope for wealth. In contrast, withdrawal, passivity, de-escalation, naturalness, and silence feel like the opposite of hope. They are, however, ways that many habitual non-protestors use to effect change.

The advice in this book will read in places, especially to habitual activists, as a kind of mysticizing attempt to get the kids off the lawn. This book recommends various kinds of behaviors generally portrayed as being exactly what those in power would like to see from a subservient populace. Of course, if you think that this is terrible advice, just what "they" want, then you should not take it.

But sometimes it really is a good idea to get off the lawn—for your own interests, not the interests of the old man doing the yelling. I think that after years of protest, some in the current wave of new activists might be ready to hear this, having realized that things are not turning out the way they might have expected and wondering why. I also think that a much larger number of readers, both students and those long past their schooldays, want to make positive change in the world but sense that the traditional protest march and rally are not always the best way to achieve that change. This book is more for them than it is for the die-hard activists who already have their preferred way of conquering the world.

4

This book has five complementary parts, each very different in style from the others.

The first, very brief section is a list of "Activism Dao's and Daon'ts" that sums up the practical advice of this book in as clear and concise a list as possible. Providing such a list is itself thoroughly un-Daoist: the notion that a certain way of working in the world can be reduced to a schematic set of instructions is an idea that ancient Daoist texts attack. However, twenty-first-century readers deserve a précis that distills much of the book into a straightforward format that can be easily referenced.

The second section is a straightforward essay, "How to Fight Fascism Lying Down." Although written in a very personal and somewhat fragmented style, the goal of this essay is to set out a clear case for why high-conflict approaches to making social change rarely work and low-conflict approaches are often a better option. This essay draws not only on my personal experience, but also on lessons from Chinese history written in ways that should be accessible to readers without any knowledge of China. Chinese people have had to live under authoritarian governments for millennia and have evolved deeply rooted survival techniques as well as wisdom for making positive change in systems where power has been removed from them. Americans need to learn from that history: we are still relying on the techniques of democratic change making to persuade an imperial imbecile who does not care about elections, legitimacy, or laws.

The third section, "The Activist" has the same title as this book as a whole because it is the original core of the book, where I began writing. In form, it is a complete rewriting and reconception of the original text of the *Daodejing* (or *Tao Te Ching*, the first Daoist book) to transform it into a protest manual. It is not a new translation—the *Daodejing* is by some estimates the fourth-most-translated book of all time, so there's no need to translate it yet again. Instead, this section is completely faithless to the original: all eighty-one chapters of the original version are here somewhere, but they've been chopped up, mixed up, souped up, and rejiggered to make them fit in a twenty-first-century context and to draw explicit connections to an activist context. In addition, those rewritten original sections have been supplemented with a large amount of new, original material in which I've done my best to channel the spirit of the author, Laozi (or Lao-tzu), to make clearer the ideas themselves and their relevance to activism.

The fourth section, "Master of the Encampment," is a rewriting and remixing of excerpts from the second great book of Daoism, the *Zhuangzi* (or Chuang Tzu); the goal of this reconception has also been to let the text directly address making change inside and outside of protest culture. Insofar as it is also a complete revision of an ancient Chinese text, this section is, therefore, much like the previous one—but it has significant differences. The *Zhuangzi* is much less known outside of China than the *Daodejing*, but its influence on Chinese civilization has been enormous. It is much, much longer than the *Daodejing*, so I have not tried to rewrite it in its entirety. It is also very different from the *Daodejing* in style and structure: unlike the bloodless and ghostly gnomic style of the *Daodejing*, the *Zhuangzi* is a book of crazed allegorical anecdotes written in a loopy literary style. It is just as irrepressibly weird as the *Daodejing*, but it's a much different weirdness—jokier, more punning, and readier to mock philosophical positions it opposes. Its author, Zhuang Zhou, can be thought of as the court jester of early Chinese philosophy—and I personally fell into his honeyed head a long time ago. So, in this section, I've tried to channel that jester voice, throwing up allegory after allegory and swapping out puns that work well in Chinese for some that work well in English. In addition, because the *Zhuangzi* regularly attributes philosophical speeches not only to allegorical figures and to mythological characters but also to Chinese historical personages who would have said nothing like what is attributed to them, I've also put words into the mouths of all kinds of Western historical figures. In no sense should any of these attributed speeches be considered actual assertions of what those figures truly believed; they are used here as literary images to drive home a point.

The final section is a short, nontechnical essay about the history of Daoism and how it relates to the very thin tradition of public protest in China. This is meant to provide more context for what Daoism has been in China than I can offer in this introduction, so that I can be up-front with readers about how the ideas in this book both draw from real Chinese traditions and in what ways this book goes beyond the claims of historical Daoism. Readers who are more interested in how to resist Trump than in ancient Chinese history can treat this section as an optional appendix, but I still hope that at least some readers will find it worth their time. History has figured large in public discussions of resistance to Trump—but only certain kinds of history, such as Timothy Snyder's very visible and excellent warnings about the rise of fascism. But histories are multiple, with divergent possibilities of lessons one could draw from them. The world has seen many brutal authoritarian leaders and many different modes of resistance to those leaders. The more models we have to think through our options, the more likely that we can see clearly what is possible and what isn't. Of course, even in that final section I can only offer a very brief sketch of some relevant portions of the history of Daoism and Chinese social movements, so at the end of the book I have added a short, annotated bibliography of good introductory books on Chinese history and Daoism for those inspired to learn more.

5

The advice I offer throughout this book is meant to be general, making the case for resistance that looks nothing like our public discourse around social activism. That's partially because it is so counterintuitive that nonresistance could sometimes be better than resistance in conquering entrenched injustice that I need to make a very foundational case. And it is partially because one of the foundational mental habits of Daoism is to oppose categorizing and technical thinking—no algorithm exists for behavior that will produce correct results so long as one follows it strictly. The complexity of the world is so deep that rules will not work—one must guide one's behavior in engaged presence with the world as it presents itself at any moment.

As a result, little in this book is a list of practical how-tos for protestors—other than the very general, overarching "Dao's and Daon'ts" list at the beginning. Part of the thesis of this very loosely structured book is that tactics and planning are overrated in achieving goals of lasting value. However, for those who just need to know what to bring to a march besides water and sunscreen, plenty of such lists reside online. Many other books offer deeper dives into protest tactics and organizing; Saul Alinsky's *Rules for Radicals* might be the most infamous, but plenty of less controversial, more contemporary rulebooks are in print.

Also missing here is any scholarship about what makes for successful protests. As a scholar writing a nonscholarly book, I know my limits. Chenoweth and Stephan's *Why Civil Resistance Works* is a good place to start for those who wish a more scholarly, evidence-based set of conclusions—and some of what they say contradicts some of what I say. But this book really isn't meant to be social science—as you'll see on reading it. This is as much about perceptual experience and distinguishing ultimate from proximate goals as about what "works," and those kinds of questions don't lend themselves well to narrowly defined datasets.

6

When scholars of Daoism see books loosely invoking Daoism for a general readership, we tend to roll our eyes. Most books with titles in the form of "The Tao of X" are bullshit: Laozi never wanted to offer you tips about your investment strategy, or about engineering design, or about horse whispering, or about country music. However, Laozi also definitely never wanted to offer anyone tips on how to run a protest movement, advocate for democratic change, or fight for fair working conditions. So, I owe it to all readers, scholars or otherwise, to say a word here about why I am going all in on the much-ridiculed practice of taking Daoism out of context. Is this book also bullshit?

It is true that many books invoke Daoism way too loosely, without a clear idea of what the Dao is or how Daoist ideas developed in ancient China. However, it is much easier to identify what Daoism isn't than to say clearly what it is. That is because, from the very beginnings of the Daoist tradition, it has been internally multiple, with sometimes-conflicting ideas being pieced together from different sources.

Laozi, the supposed founder of Daoism, likely never existed: the *Daodejing* has all the hallmarks of a text that evolved through many authors, including in oral folk transmission. The *Zhuangzi* and other early Daoist texts combine chapters from different authors, and scholars spend enormous effort trying to tease apart which strands of received text derive from which original sources. Plenty of non-Daoist texts of the earlier period borrowed liberally from Daoism, especially when turning it into more heavily political or strategic use (see the final essay in this volume for more details). The creation of two Daoist religious movements in the late second century AD was a massive departure from the incipiently philosophical texts that had emerged four centuries previously; it is very hard to say that the theology of the Celestial Masters sect is more faithful to the *Daodejing* than is, say, *The Tao of Pooh*. There are some definite and real commonalities to Daoist thought across texts and movements in early China, but even the most commonly seen elements are very difficult to reduce to a core of essential teachings that appear in every Daoist text. The word "authentic," therefore, doesn't have much meaning when it comes to judging whether a given text should or shouldn't be considered Daoist. A perfect original ideal against which to compare later adaptations never existed.

One way to think about this is to call shenanigans on the whole thing; to say that Daoism has always been bullshit. Another way of describing this tradition, probably better, is to say that it has always been flexible, creative, and experimental, not particularly concerned with orthodox tenets, and willing to strike out in unexpected directions when circumstances warrant. The maddening variation that results from this constant evolution is exactly what one would expect: among the closest thing to core, inviolable beliefs of philosophical Daoism is a belief that beliefs should be held lightly. One should go with the flow of the world as it is, change unceasingly with the changes in one's environment, and deconstruct the categories that the world thinks are orthodox. There's a sense, then, in which departures from the ideas of the *Daodejing* and the *Zhuangzi* are more "authentic" to Daoism than would be scholarly attempts to restate in boundary enslaved exactitude what the original founders of the tradition had in mind.

This book is not a work of scholarship that would obligate me to specific, correct postulates about what ancient texts claimed. It is an attempt to flow toward something entirely new from within the living river of Daoist philosophy. Because I have published a fair amount of scholarly work on this tradition, I feel confident to innovate in a way that feels faithful to the way Daoism has always innovated, constantly departing from itself. It doesn't much matter to me that no ancient Daoist text ever had anything to say about social activism—this text is a performance of what might have been said, in an offshoot of Daoism that evolved in ways similar to all the other offshoots.

So, this book isn't "authentic" Daoism, but it's inauthentic to Daoism in the way that Daoists have always been inauthentic. Although no one authentic version of Daoism exists, readers who would like a clearer grasp on the historical particularities of various ancient texts and sects are warmly encouraged to start with one of the books in the suggestions for additional reading listed in the concluding pages.

7

A sign of fidelity by infidelity to Daoism is the ingestion of foreign materials. Early Daoist texts are graphophages, sliding over and encompassing and digesting things that originally were their own free-swimming intellectual paramecia in the currents of Chinese thought. This is how yin-yang theory (and the "yin-yang symbol") associated with Daoism. It is how the hexagrams of the *Classic of*

Changes (or *Yijing/I Ching*) associated with Daoism. And it is even how the word *dao* itself associated with Daoism. Each of these famished incorporations into the body of the tradition occurred to allow writers, literati, and prophets to reach out to contemporaries and make their points relevant within a shifting sociohistorical context.

When I decided to write this book by reperforming Daoist moves rather than recopying Daoist tenets, I knew that I had to let loose my inner Pac-Man and gobble into this book every reference that made sense. Unlike Warring States–era Chinese editors, I did not lift whole sentences or paragraphs from other books and reprint them here without attribution: one of the realities of my context is copyright law and anti-plagiarism norms, and I have retained enough scholarly self-control to observe those strictly. But allusions everywhere throughout the central two sections came neither from the *Daodejing* nor the *Zhuangzi*. Some of these are allusions to Chinese texts—and I've sneaked in a few quick translations of medieval poetry and scriptures, as Easter eggs for those with deeper familiarity with Chinese literature. However, because I am writing for an English-reading audience, a fair number of allusions are to texts originally written in English or familiar to English readers.

When I was very young, I learned a special crayon technique. By rubbing many different colors intensely over the same patch of paper, layering scribble upon heavy scribble, textures began to emerge from the hued deposits. These retained the kaleidoscopic mix of whichever colors one had laid down, eventually forming a rainbow wax brocade. The whole might look a sort of neutral muddle, but close inspection with a finger laid over the area revealed a sparkling and thick complexity—a tot's pointillism. That effect is sometimes seen in the form of books written by people who have read too much, without the corresponding level of writerly craft to make actual art out of literary pastiche. I suspect it is what readers who care about form might find here in this book, palely. It isn't a way of writing that wows, but I hope it weaves at least the rough pleasure of something mildly textured and simple.

8

Since the early twentieth century, one popular way of being creatively inauthentic to Daoism in the West has been to pitch it as a kind of woo-woo mysticism for the cultural left, a way to explore spirituality without yielding to the strictures and repressive superstition of organized religion. In China, the associations with the belief system are nearly opposite—Daoism is often thought of by the Chinese urban middle class as a form of superstition practiced by semiliterate peasants. In part, that is due to what has crossed borders: the *Daodejing* and a few other early Daoist texts that might have some metaphysical assumptions, but that also have philosophical points to make, have been translated and disseminated broadly. The later versions of Daoism that, starting in the second century AD, developed into hierarchical religions with their own pantheons of gods, church structures, and canons of moral and ritual requirements stayed in China, with little influence abroad.

However, it is hard to read the *Daodejing* and conclude that there isn't something mystical going on, even if it is very hard to pin down exactly what its metaphysical claims might be. This book replicates that feeling of "something mystical" throughout, but that does not mean that it is trying to advance or support any kind of theological claims.

Setting aside the most likely intentions of early Daoist texts as determined by scholarship, it certainly is possible to read those texts as advocating traditional psychological practices, very loosely defined forms of meditation in which one seeks to rid oneself of sensory distraction and to focus on more placid visions of the world. Advice in this book, and the vision of the universe it describes, should similarly be taken in a metaphysically noncommittal sense: nothing here is intended to conflict with either the most strictly materialist atheism or the most conservative versions of the Abrahamic faiths. I am not even claiming—beyond the level of metaphor—that nontheological meditation is necessary or helpful. What this book does say is that effective action for social good requires the ability to rid oneself, at a very deep level, of certain commonplace habits of thought that promote conflict. If either meditation or connection to their own religious beliefs or practices would be helpful for some readers in practicing the advice here, they certainly should feel free to do so; but no one should feel that this is required to understand or use this book.

9

One of the major themes of early Daoism, replicated in this book, is suspicion of language as being insufficient to communicate the fullness of the way things are. This isn't really a statement that language cannot say things that are true: "true" and "false" are words that describe other words. Rather, Daoist suspicion of language is deeper than that, suggesting that language never can adequately describe reality. In the *Daodejing*, this suspicion is primarily directed at the word *Dao*, the Way, a thing that exists somehow beyond all experience at the conceptual source of the world. In later Daoist writings, especially the *Zhuangzi*, the ability of language to describe anything, even the common objects of experience, is called into question.

Imagine taking a photo of an unremarkable path through the woods, when leaves have just returned, and the ground is still muddy and chilled. You could not capture in words the information contained in that photo. Even if you could speak the language of machines, and narrate in code, line by line, the exact color of each pixel of a jpeg, you still would not be able to describe fully the way each section of color seemed to play off against each other section of color, how areas of light and shade combined and parted, the exact titrations of blur and clarity that would frame even a dull mood about that average path in an unexciting spring. The reason for this is that human language is a low-information-density code, and our language-processing systems have low bandwidth. If we had evolved with built-in Wi-Fi, we would have developed more efficient codes than English or Chinese. As we are stuck with language, we must muddle through with systems that can only describe reality very indirectly and with very low resolution, through generalization and metaphor.

However, if language is such a poor code, why use it at all, rather than collapsing into silence? Why have I written a book lauding silence, rather than just keeping my thoughts to myself?

No perfect strategy exists to move off from hypocrisy if one wishes to use words to accuse words. Both analytical and Continental philosophy have developed very sophisticated, specialized ways of making those arguments. Written for people rather than for specialist scholars, the texts of early Daoism take other approaches: the *Daodejing* is vague, absent, and mystifying, whereas the *Zhuangzi* is punning, playful, and self-satirizing. In every literary tradition, poetry has sometimes tried to show what lies beyond the reach of words by ginning up words to their most saturated, hotheaded point.

I've tried to use all these strategies in this book. Hopefully, it will get the point across, but I don't lay claim to any kind of logical consistency. On the plus side, that also limits the insanity of my demands: nothing in here should be understood as saying that one must literally take a permanent vow of silence to be an effective activist.

10

I am not Chinese. Because this is a very political book, deeply influenced by a tradition to which, in important ways, I will always be an outsider, I owe both Chinese and non-Chinese readers some self-reflection about my own status and position in writing a book like this.

Many readers are perhaps unfamiliar with the realities of ancient or modern China but have much greater familiarity with ethnic-studies discourse in the United States and Canada. According to the ways that minority cultural rights are discussed in English, my position as a white man seemingly appropriating a Chinese cultural tradition probably appears suspect. It's a reasonable suspicion. I don't think it would be a great act of anti-racism to say that white writers should never be influenced by non-Western sources, and if people are so scared of being charged with cultural appropriation that they devote themselves to promoting always and only the European canon, that would be a massive failure of cultural politics. Nonetheless, as a writer who cannot claim Chinese traditions as any kind of birthright, I do owe readers an explanation of why I think this book honors rather than steals.

On the most general level, one should always evaluate appropriation through cultural and historical context. The situation of China is incredibly different from the situation of, for example, North American Indigenous peoples, who have had to experience histories of genocide, colonialism, and predation in which those peoples' cultural relics and traditions have been stolen and profited from by white society. Chinese people face global hostility, and anti-Asian racism is sadly thriving in North America, but the barriers faced by those communities are not identical to those faced by others. Just as important, the position of Chinese American communities that continue to face real racism and exclusion within the context of a majority-white America is not the same position as that of China, the world superpower, which isn't taking anybody's shit. One part of understanding and celebrating difference, and respectful engagement with non-Western cultures, is to understand at a deep level the fact of difference between those various communities and not to apply a one-size-fits-all approach. My act of writing here, under the influence of Chinese philosophy and the hope to spread that influence further, is not meant to steal anything from China but to pay homage.

A key to thinking through China's foreign cultural engagements is to understand that both in ancient times and in the twenty-first century, Chinese leaders and intellectuals have usually viewed the foreign dissemination of Chinese culture as an unalloyed good. Chinese policymakers have always sought to promote the adoption of Chinese cultural landmarks and standards by non-Chinese peoples because this process has been seen as encouraging foreign sympathies with the Chinese state and allowing expansion of Chinese spheres of influence. In ancient times, this process was called "transformation of the barbarians"; now it is called, in international relations argot, "soft power."

The current government of the People's Republic of China has all kinds of programs to promote foreign appreciation for, engagement with, and even appropriation of Chinese culture. The most famous of these are the Confucius Institutes, which are really just cultural centers akin to those of France's "Alliance Française" or Germany's "Goethe-Institut," not the spy networks that xenophobes imagine. Programs also exist to increase translation of Chinese works into foreign languages, generous scholarships to promote study in China, funding for arts exchanges, and so on. Nor is all this simply a cynical ploy by the Chinese government; it is common for average Chinese people to welcome foreigners' attainment of linguistic and cultural fluency. Although Chinese American communities sometimes have very reasonable concerns about certain kinds of cultural appropriation, in China fluent non-native speakers are celebrated on television variety shows, where they frequently are dressed in traditional Chinese costumes without any charges of cultural appropriation; and they generally receive warm receptions everywhere they go.

Moreover, all three of China's major traditional belief systems—Confucianism, Daoism, and Buddhism—are all fundamentally transnational in deep historical ways. Daoism is the belief that brought the language of "transformation of the barbarians" to the forefront of Chinese international relations theory. One legend held that Laozi at the end of his life left China to travel westward and eventually ended up in India, where he was named "Buddha," so Buddhism could be seen (in medieval interfaith polemics) as a bastardized form of Daoism. In more recent times, the *Daodejing* is an incredibly internationalized text: it is usually listed as the world's fourth-most-translated book. Like most of the great world philosophies and religions, it has a known origin point, but it has spread to adherents of many ethnic backgrounds, who have appropriated and localized it. Daoism and Buddhism have had a major countercultural influence on writers in the United States and Canada since at least the early 1960s. Hence, I'm here appropriating a tradition that has long since been acknowledged as belonging first to China, but also to world literature, that already in a sense has been nativized in North America.

Of course, if you think I'm still doing something wrong here in this book, and you would prefer to read the original *Daodejing* and *Zhuangzi*, please do! As a scholar who loves the original work and an educator dedicated to promoting understanding of China, I would be delighted if dissatisfied readers wanted to go back to the source. There will never be a replacement for the riches of Chinese literary civilization, and I certainly don't pretend that this book is any kind of substitute.

11

Some, reading this book, will find that it drains hope out of the possibility of protest. If so, that is a good, productive thing. Hope distorts and misleads, reducing the effectiveness of movements for social change. This is not to say that the book intends to promote despair. Despair also distorts and misleads, and it is just as useless as hope.

It would be better to say that this book is intended to give readers the tools to liberate themselves from both hope and despair; to see the world as it is, and both to act and to refrain from acting in ways that will be most effective. In service to that liberation, I have tried to deconstruct a great deal of the architecture of activism, and some will read that deconstruction as a personal attack or as a stalking horse for entrenched interests that fight to prevent change.

In fact, the advice in this book greatly expands the means and scope for effective social change. By canceling the monopoly of well-trained protest-centric activism over change, we could license anyone to make positive work for good an effect of their being in the world while reducing the harms that ensue from ill-considered activism. We do not need to use the crutch of hope to draw people into the streets if we can be more effective by rarely going out into the streets.

In sending this book on its way, though, I will allow myself one small hope. For those who have never found the need or the ability to be loud and confrontational in the service of justice, I hope that you find here confirmation that you were never a bad or a cowardly person. You may have been following the true course toward progress all along.

Activism Dao's and Daon'ts

Ancient Daoist texts advocate against simplified moral codes, so this list of things one should and should not do in trying to better the world is extremely un-Daoist in form. Nonetheless, this book (like genuine ancient Daoist texts) does advance certain discrete ideas and claims, and these can be put into list format. As this book is very weird and difficult in places, and as I wrote it to be a potential resource for people who wish to do good in the world, it is fair that I offer this list as a simple reference guide for readers who need a distillation of the book's advice. Please just hold this section lightly; ultimately, learning a certain way of seeing the world and being in it are more useful to activism—and to living—than any codified list of what to do and not to do. Learning that course of seeing and being is the most important thing to "Dao."

Activism Dao's

- Be content to do nothing when nothing will work.
- Avoid conflict.
- Maximize gains by minimizing effort.
- Use language to build relationships.
- Stay out of the public eye.

- Act locally and think locally.
- Stay small.
- Be quiet.
- Care for yourself, not about yourself.
- Ground yourself in mystery.
- See your opponents as "us," not as "them."
- Recognize the true state of things with no illusions.
- Chase what is possible.
- Address those with power to make change.
- Go straight at the goal.
- Harmonize relentlessly.
- Let opponents overreact.
- Preserve spontaneity.
- Prioritize direct action over politics.
- Ignore this list when the situation demands it.

Activism Daon'ts

- Do something just because you can.
- Feel you must act.
- Let emotion determine your direction.
- Create conflict.

- Force a response.
- Assume anger can be nonviolent.
- Center yourself and your feelings.
- Use slogans
- Convey clear demands.
- Trust language.
- Take the bait.
- Pressure from the outside.
- Put media first.
- Put social media first.
- Demonize or endanger anyone.
- Target whomever happens to be closest.
- Trust ideologies.
- Trust past examples.
- Overreact.
- Let tactics obscure strategy.
- Save the world.
- Chase heroism.
- Prioritize politics over direct action.
- Take this list as immutable.

Activism Checklist
Only take a specific action if it meets all these criteria:

Action Criteria	☑
This action has a clear and achievable goal.	☐
You can see a specific pathway by which this action will result in change.	☐
No neutral parties will feel harmed or threatened by this action.	☐
You understand clearly how this action will be seen outside your group.	☐
This action does not rely on media or social media to be effective.	☐
Any less-conflictual and less-public actions have been tried first.	☐
The action is aimed at those with the power to make change.	☐
The action is likely to build bridges to groups that disagree with you.	☐
Of all possible actions, this one best minimizes effort and maximizes gain.	☐
You have a clear strategy for preserving the health and safety of all involved.	☐
You are acting based on the needs of others, not your psychological needs.	☐

How to Fight Fascism
Lying Down

1

It was a crisp day of red leaves in 1996 when I thought to damn nature and raise the dead.

I was living in a Beijing exurb where agricultural labor bordered on the governmental and educational economy of the capital. Sweet smoke from roadside roasted yam vendors would always line my route home from work to an apartment compound on the far side of several blocks of migrant labor housing. The smell of smoky Beijing autumn still comes back to me whenever I see the word "invigorate"; recalling those leaning shack alleys through the haze is harder.

The coal smoke was unusually heavy one day when I approached some sort of disturbance. I could see that it was a large group of several dozen people agitated and huddling near the side entrance of the University of Politics and Law, so my first thought was that it was some sort of protest.

As I approached closer, I could see what it really was: a dead child, six or seven, laid out upon a small flatbed trailer and surrounded by a large, gawking crowd. Later, I learned that the child had died from carbon monoxide poisoning, sleeping next to a coal furnace in one of the poorly ventilated huts. I could not quite tell who were the child's parents and who were slightly more distant relatives or other neighbors, but the sound of grief was hanging thick and greasy in the air. Around the most touched mourners were extended circles of concerned neighbors and idle bystanders—I was the idlest, and the farthest in orbit around the child.

This was a time in my life when I was manic with God. I had just converted to a version of Christianity that was weird in ecstasy and reading, hanging uncomfortably somewhere between Calvin's Institutes, sweaty and tract-laden street preachers, and fourth-century desert monophysite hermits. Having expected something of political significance and seeing instead a sudden and immense personal tragedy, displayed on the street like persimmons on a market cart, something went wrong inside me. For the longest single minute of my life, I was seized by a mania, impelled by a thought to raise the boy back to life. I was not schizophrenic; I knew that I had no such power. Yet the thought seized me that the death of such a boy was unacceptable, so I would not accept it. I ought to be able, through some combination of faith, willpower, and sincerity, to wake him up again. I was not conscious of my own whiteness or my stumbling Mandarin; my entire consciousness was on the wrongness of what I saw and the need to correct it.

I did not take even one step toward the boy on his industrial bier, and the mania passed. Coming back to reality, I saw my own powerlessness to fix anything, and I accepted it. Had I tried to revive the child—or even simply gone over to express condolences to the family—I would only have caused greater pain, inserting myself into a mourning process where I did not belong. So, I kept walking.

Few protest movements would be as utterly hopeless as an attempt at freelance resurrection, but many come very close. The Chinese state, backed by the largest military and the most comprehensive internal security structures on Earth, will never be toppled by student protests. Attempting to topple it can only cause harm. Therefore, it is imperative to see reality clearly and act accordingly.

That goes for all protest movements: to have any hope of success, they must work with the grain of reality, not against it. Inspirations and ideologies that try to perform miracles will instead perform pain.

2

Chairman Mao was a good poet. He was not a great poet—while his contemporaries were inventing thick or frank or gnarled versions of Chinese poetic modernism, Mao was too stuck in a masculine Romantic mode. But he did have an excellent grasp of traditional poetic idiom, sufficient to innovate away from trite and inexpressive stock phrases while staying in classical forms. One of his most famous early poems reads, in part:

> Eagles slap the long and empty sky,
> fish soar down amid the shallow deeps,
> all beings fight for freedom below the skies of frost.
> Aghast at the vastness,
> I demand of the empyrean and the land,
> "Who masters the sinking, and the rising?"

Four decades after writing these lines, when it was Mao who mastered the sinking and the rising, he sent millions to their deaths. His crimes were different than those of a Hitler or a Stalin: he was not genocidal. But he had a vision of sweeping the masses into a certain new order, designed with the clear, straight lines of ideology upon the ground of an old society that had to be bulldozed down to nothing. The vision was grand and unconstrained, masculine and Romantic, and it was too aesthetically seductive in its vision of a possible world to be bothered with the gristle of individual bodies.

When poets become the acknowledged legislators of the world, run.

3

I have always protested through my eyes, not on my feet.

My introduction to live protests were those centered in Tiananmen Square in the weeks before the massacre on June 4, 1989. Those protests were on nightly, on the little thirteen-inch black-and-white TV that we kept in the kitchen. I would do my homework at the kitchen table, where my parents could see me, but I kept the TV on, and I was watching the scene in the square, hour after hour, on into the night.

I don't think any of us ever understand what it was like to live through our parents' histories, and I don't think my own daughter understands the air of the late 1980s. I'm sure that most of my students don't. For Americans who had grown up under a seemingly eternal overhang of nuclear war, it was a sort of spiritual spring in which threat could be lifted from afar. Reagan-Gorbachev summits yielded to more radical changes: unrest in the Caucasus, independence in the Baltics, elections in Moscow. It spread across eastern Europe and beyond. The fall of the Berlin Wall. No more USSR. It was hard not to be happy at having no more enemies. I was not a committed capitalist. I was a teenager who wanted a future.

In the middle of that motion, the events that circled around the eye of Tiananmen were among the most spectacular. I knew a few things about China: it was huge, it was socialist, and it was nuclear; but it was also moving in the direction of openness and friendship, and it had been for a decade. More importantly, the protests were televised live, on and on for weeks. The great Sino-Soviet summit between Deng Xiaoping and Mikhail Gorbachev had brought foreign television crews into Beijing, where they began showing the protests that had already been surging for a month. A hundred thousand students were in the square, speaking, reading, debating democracy and economic justice, going on hunger strikes, and eventually building a great indigenized Statue of Liberty, towering forth with her own Chinese torch. And the foreign cameras just rolled on and on.

The last time I was in the square, more than a decade ago, I showed my daughter the Public Security Bureau cameras attached to every lamppost and told her quietly why we had to behave.

4

The story of how China went from press cameras to security cameras is a story of collective choices. It is possible, especially from a Chinese perspective, to see these as exactly the right choices: China is now wealthy, powerful, feared, and at peace. It has already passed the United States in technological and economic leadership, and it will be the indispensable nation of the twenty-first century. But because China's choices have built such success, it remains important to remember their cost: hundreds killed, thousands imprisoned or self-exiled, nights spent staring at nothing, a generation lost to idolatry of cash and state. But it is not the place of non-Chinese people to judge whether that road was worth that cost.

What it is anybody's place to dwell on is the social-science phenomenon of the collectivity of the choices. The days in which the army rolled into Beijing were a time of grief and rage for the residents of Beijing, and even the little ripples of that trauma that reached me, safe in suburban New York, sufficed for a faint despair. In those days, it was easy to see the deaths and the voiding of resistance as the brutal choice of Deng Xiaoping, guided by his hatchet man, Premier Li Peng. It could not be explained well to those of us who watched from the outside, with no good grasp of Chinese history: China had been opening, as the world had been opening. Deng had seemed a partial friend. And then—the violence.

What I learned later was that although Deng could have made a choice not to follow through with a bloody crackdown and ensuing repression, that choice was made much harder by the choices of the protestors. They had been given numerous off-ramps. They could have gone home after the funeral of Hu Yaobang, the erstwhile beloved general secretary whose death had catalyzed discontent into protest. They could have gone home after the seventieth anniversary of the May Fourth protests—a turning point in Chinese modernity in which students had rallied for science and democracy. They could have gone home after Zhao Ziyang (Hu Yaobang's successor, and the students' primary ally in the government) came and begged them to go home. There were factions who did want to leave. There were ridiculous struggles for power, and miniature leadership coups that amounted to stealing and re-stealing the bullhorns used for speeches. But the last decampments only happened when the tanks had reached the very edge of the square, and by then it was too late—the course that had to be run had already been chosen. Not cracking down on the protests might not have led to a reactionary coup against Deng, but did he know that? Did he know that the intelligence reports he was receiving about CIA manipulation of the students were xenophobic misreadings of bland American consular visits? The longer the students stayed, and the more radical and uncompromising their demands became, the more they increased internal pressures on Deng to choose martial law.

Had they disbanded when the tanks had begun to circle Beijing, fewer would have gone to prison, and the extreme censorship and surveillance apparatus that followed would have been lighter and looser. Had they left when Zhao Ziyang begged, he might have escaped sacking, and a reform space in the government could have survived. Had they left after the May Fourth anniversary, they would have established a patriotic brand and built a possibility of more intellectual ferment. Had they left after Hu Yaobang's funeral, his faction would have been strengthened, and more space would have been claimed for safe dissent. At each stage of persistence, the protestors shrank the space of what they could achieve and widened the space for potential disaster. And yet at each stage, they became more and more convinced that uncompromising strength would somehow force down the immense Chinese state. They became the mirror image of the government in stubbornness—but the People's Liberation Army kept all the tanks.

I did not understand this later, until after I had learned Chinese, learned the modern history of China, and watched many more protests in other places fail in the same way. Now I do not understand why it was ever hard to see and why it is still hard to see for each new generation, all around the world, that discovers its very own self-destructive voice.

5

Protests have a kind of pattern that is hard to fully capture in words. One must stand by them, and watch them, and see the manifold of nature unfold according to its own process and in its own time. It is like watching a cloud of small birds far off, twisting and bulging rhythmically in the air as it tries to determine a direction.

The patterns of nature hold for protests, too, because humans are also a swarm, and we have our own mathematically complex but predictable group dynamics. Unlike birds, it is hard to watch ourselves that way because we are inside our own cloud, pulled by our own evolved programming to maintain our own speed and distance from our neighbors. Our motions run on calculated interest, but also upon the grasping and distracting insistence of our emotions. Greed, fear, love, pride, and disgust all send us tracing different paths of conflict and evasion—each of us making our own way by our own innate sense, and by those logics replicating the same patterns. This is how generations pass on, one to the next, handing down our mistakes like heirlooms of the species.

These dynamics rule at all scales but cannot be observed well at all scales. A nation is too large. A family is too small, and too private—unless it is your own, and then there is no objectivity. But protests are usually at the right scale for naturalistic observation. This is why I watch them, in scopophilic perversion, from their margins. I show up and loiter, like an unwashed predator at a playground. I see and stay unseen, hear but stay unheard.

6

Some protest movements are successful. The Indian independence movement and the American Civil Rights Movement are two that everyone knows. Women's suffrage movements everywhere. South Africa's anti-apartheid movement. Post-Stonewall gay rights movements. On smaller scales, thousands of tiny local protests successfully get parking ordinances overturned or popular teachers rehired.

Most protests are not successful. Some fizzle out; many backfire spectacularly. Anti–Vietnam War protests elected Nixon. The Arab Spring, in most countries, either devolved into chaos or was met with brutal repression. The Prague Spring led straight to Soviet tanks. The 2019 Hong Kong protests led to the removal of the last vestiges of Hong Kong autonomy within China. Student protests of the war in Gaza have led to massive defunding of America's great universities.

Even a spectacularly successful protest can turn suddenly into disaster. The protests that evolved quickly into the storming of the Bastille turned into a successful revolution, which led to the Terror, which led to military dictatorship, which led to the devastation of Europe.

7

So why protest?

Protests are hard tasks. They exact enormous opportunity costs. They take an emotional toll. Protestors must know that their chances of success are low, even if they do not understand that they may not want the success that they seek.

Many respect the sacrifice of those who are die-hard, committed activists from well-off families, sacrificing their privilege to enact change. I have respect for the opposite: those who would prefer to live their private lives but are driven onto the streets in hunger or in war, because they have nothing left to lose. They are more honest. They need to win. They gain no satisfaction from having done their part.

Those who choose to protest, having the privilege of a choice, care. I am sure that they care at the center of their conscious minds. I am not sure that every one of them cares at the edges or under the surface. Have you ever heard someone say, "I don't want to be the kind of person who sees this tragedy and does nothing"? I have heard it said, again and again, and it causes the inside of my rib cage to itch. The person who says this might not, in their innermost core, want to fix the problem; perhaps they want to see themselves as a certain kind of person. The desire to mount the stage and act a role for an audience of oneself is powerful. If it were effective at making positive change, who could complain? A child alive because of vanity is a living child.

The problem is that protesting for the wrong reason leads to the wrong protest dynamics and the wrong result. Acting a role can be deadly.

8

The road to the Tiananmen massacre began with a telegenic and disastrous act of role-playing.

The state funeral for the beloved Hu Yaobang, the erstwhile reformer, was held in the Great Hall of the People, the home of the Chinese legislature, on the morning of April 22. Sitting on the western edge of Tiananmen square, the Great Hall is a massive block of socialist architecture, with a flight of steps leading up to it from the open expanse of the public space. State leaders had gathered inside, with thousands of students in the square below, and the ceremony progressed to its end.

When it had finished, three student leaders marched halfway up the stairs with a petition that they wanted to present to Premier Li Peng. They then knelt, heads down in supplication, with the leader's arms outstretched, holding out the petition as an offering.

Everyone understood this pose, deeply woven into traditional Chinese political culture. It was the pose of the loyalist Confucian official whose behavior was a central ideal inculcated through the educational system and replicated in the actions of high-minded high ministers, dynasty after dynasty and century after century. In the Confucian system of political philosophy, the official has a duty of petition and remonstrance toward the sovereign, so long as the sovereign is willing to listen. This duty should be acted out from a place of submission, accepting and acknowledging the ruler's supremacy in the state and willing to accept the risks of telling the truth to a man with unchecked power over life and death.

By kneeling with the petition held out in front of them, upward toward the gaggle around Li Peng, the students were playing the role of loyalist Confucian officials. In their own eyes, and in the eyes of the students below throughout the square, they were demonstrating loyalty and humility, submission and patriotism. While asking for reforms in line with international understandings of democratic rights, they were doing so in the most classically Chinese way possible. It was meant as a gesture of fealty to the state and patriotic loyalty to China, dispelling any notion that begging for democracy was a CIA-led subversion. But the students did not think about how playing this role would appear to the government ministers whom they sought to persuade.

Li Peng was not the emperor of a Chinese dynasty. He was the premier of the People's Republic of China, coming out of the Great Hall of the People. The monumentality of that building, and its elevation from ground level, signified the greatness of the people and the legitimacy of the Communist Party as the voice of the people. By playing their self-assigned roles as premodern Confucian officials, the students were forcing Li Peng to play instead the role of a premodern emperor—in other words, to deny the entire basis of the government's claimed legitimacy in popular sovereignty. Their position on the stairs made the action worse, because it replicated the structure of imperial courts, where the emperor would sit on a throne raised on steps above the audience hall. Suddenly, they had converted the entire stone edifice of socialist architecture into a trap, framing Li in a space of hypocritical absolutist power. And he had no good option: if he accepted the petition, he would appear to accept the framing; if he rejected the petition, he would appear to be brutal and uncaring. Eventually, a guard was sent to take the document and shoo the students down the stairs, but the damage was done. They had managed to publicly shame, on the biggest stage possible, the man whose support they were seeking and who would play a pivotal role in deciding their fates.

The students wanted change, but they also wanted to see themselves acting out the heroic roles that had been inculcated through their education. On April 22, that took the form of premodern Confucian cultural ideals; two weeks later, on the anniversary of May 4, it took the form of China's modern nationalist ideals. But in playing their roles, they blinded themselves to the reception they would receive. It is as if, donning a costume, one suddenly loses the basic "theory of mind" acquired by infants, the understanding that other people have their own thoughts and way of seeing the world not identical to one's own.

When I see protestors making this mistake again and again, for all causes and in all contexts, I know exactly what they are thinking—without understanding at all what they are thinking.

9

The word "polysemy" refers to the ability of symbols to carry multiple complex and shifting meanings; and the incident on the steps of the Great Hall of the People demonstrates how inescapable it is in protest. It is a difficult enough aspect of communication in literature, where the stakes are usually low, and one gets to use as many words as one wants to explain what one means. It is a much more dangerous facet of protests, which communicate through brief moments on television or simplified slogans on placards and can have life-or-death stakes.

This is all made worse by online fights. Had there been Chinese social media in 1989, the students' gesture of submissive Confucian petitioning would have immediately been subjected to a hermeneutic contest: Was it an act of respectful and loyalist patriotism? Or was it an arrogant and satirical attempt to shame the government? Outraged digital warriors would have launched into vast threads of irresolvable argument, each side marshaling both facts and vitriol, no doubt scouring the classical dynastic histories for examples and counterexamples in attempts to score points. And those arguments would have very effectively diverted focus away from students' demands for economic and political rights. In the end, the result could hardly have been any worse for the students than it was, but that is because the government decision-makers already had the worst possible opinion of what the students did. It is a different matter for protest in open and democratic societies where persuasion of elected leaders presumably is the goal.

To see how this works, we don't need to rely only on counterfactuals from China thirty-five years ago. Look at the student protests over Israeli actions in Gaza and think about how many of the on-campus and online fights that played out during 2023–2024 were about the meaning of words: "genocide," "intifada," "Zionist," "settler colonialism," "from the river to the sea." Put aside who is right or wrong in the interpretation of words such as these. Put aside whether "right" and "wrong" are themselves words that have clear, easy meanings in this context. Consider only how interpretations have been working. Palestinian students interpret these words through their own family and community histories of generational trauma, and we have no good reason to assume that they do not believe, strongly, their own interpretations. Many Jewish students interpret these words through their own very different family and community histories of generational trauma, and we have no good reason to assume that they do not believe, strongly, their own interpretations. Perhaps you think that one side or the other is insane to believe things the way they do—but they do, and when someone believes something because of the tearful stories of suffering passed down from grandparents, their minds will not be changed by shouting at rallies or online name-calling. Fights over these words cannot be won.

What fights over those words did do was to distract everyone's attention from the suffering of civilians in Gaza and refocus it on American campus culture. Take the very most-significant fight over the word "genocide," waged not on the Columbia campus but at the International Court of Justice, through the case that South Africa brought against Israel. The fight over defining genocide did not in any way force Israel to stop or to slow its military operations, because popular opinion overwhelmingly saw Hamas as an existential threat, and Israel's government judged the elimination of that threat worth any price in international condemnation or in Palestinian lives.

Fighting over the definition of "genocide" is a distraction from the piles of innocent, blasted, and starved human bodies that lie strewn around the rubble of Gaza. Does anyone think that a single child was not blown to bits because of a social media thread explaining "from the river to the sea"?

10

For nine months, I circled the edges of protests on my own campus, in my own sick weird way. I saw a lot of anger, a lot of aggression, a lot of grief, a lot of trauma. And it was in the service of—so far as I could see—nothing at all.

During that year, many editorials around the protests on many campuses celebrated students as upholding the best traditions of the university, standing up for their values and holding their respective administrations accountable. I hope that they felt good about themselves for doing so. But when I joined meetings about the protests that have happened on my own campus, I could not hear those arguments very well. I had to concentrate instead on my own most immediate need: not to vomit all over the conference table.

Was the goal really to let students stand up for their values? Was the goal really to hold the administrations accountable? Why wasn't the goal to help Gaza? How would shaking a righteous fist at our university administrations have helped Gaza? The students' most prominent demand on most campuses was to disclose and divest from Israel. Even if disinvestment were feasible, everyone—including the students—understood that other investors would come in and take the deals offered until share prices rose back up to meet market fundamentals. The most that could have been accomplished is to take a stand and say, "Not in our name!" and to keep one's own hands clean in one tiny area of the massively globalized conditions of twenty-first-century social existence.

It is too bad that refugees can't shelter in the fortress of our moral purity.

11

Knowing what not to say, and when not to say it, is the heart of persuasion.

Knowing what not to do, and when not to do it, is the core of achievement.

Had the students at Tiananmen tried to build their movement upon genuine Confucian ethics and political theory, rather than upon Confucian playacting, they would have had a better sense of what to do and what not to do. Most non-Chinese people (and quite a few modern Chinese people who aren't specialists in the history of philosophy) tend to assume that Confucianism is an insipid moralism of submission to hierarchy. Obey the king, obey your parents, obey your husband. That's a bad oversimplification. The system contains very little justification for outright rebellion against authority—but withdrawal and nonparticipation are core values. When a minister serves a good king, he should be honest and faithful. But when he serves a bad king, he should quit and move to another country.

Confucius also is responsible for inventing the key Chinese concept of "nonaction":

子曰：「無為而治者，其舜也與？夫何為哉，恭己正南面而已矣。」

Confucius said, "Wasn't [the sage-king] Shun one who governed by nonaction? All he did was to behave reverently and sit due south [upon the throne]."

The legendary king Shun was a model of governance, keeping peace and prosperity, behaving with modesty and respect for his elders. Here, Confucius attributes his success to his ability to do nothing. It is an odd and uncomfortable sentiment that was hardly less radical and difficult to practice in ancient China than it is today. How can one make a life for oneself by doing nothing? How can one advocate and act for the betterment of society through nonaction? Only a die-hard libertarian would prefer a governing authority that did nothing but sit around and look reverent.

The ancient histories that first record Shun's legendary reign do record him as having taken actions, so Confucius probably was not being literal or doctrinaire. The point is that bringing about positive social change rests more upon being a certain way in the world than upon making maximalist interventions in the social order.

12

Laozi expanded and radicalized that Confucian concept of nonaction. Later, after he had been recognized as the founder of a philosophy/religion called Daoism, people tended to forget that Confucius had mentioned nonaction first, and they came to think of it as a deeply Daoist ideal. Laozi's most famous formulation is:

無為而無不為

Do nothing, and there is nothing you do not do.

Within the context of his book, the *Daodejing*, this concept of nonaction gains a broadened scope of action. It certainly still applies to the governing style of good kings, as Confucius had attributed to Shun. It also is the (non-)behavior attributed to sages in general. And it gains a very personal use as well, so it seems to apply to all aspects of living in the world related to the book's promotion of mild asceticism and releasing the self from ambition and materialism.

This radical and confusing proposition is one of many such in the book. Other major themes include

- the misleading character of language, which imposes false categories upon the world;
- the superiority of traditionally low-status characteristics such as weakness, dullness, lowness, and femininity;

- the usefulness of uselessness;
- the origin of social virtues such as justice and charity in social failure, and the need to move beyond such virtues;
- the healthfulness of being natural and living a simple life; and
- the source of the world in something impossible to define but conceptually prior to existence: the Course (or *dao*).

Daoism is much more complex than these few themes in this one book. Modern editions of the Ming-dynasty Daoist Canon, the most comprehensive collection of Daoist writings prior to the fifteenth century, run to dozens of huge, heavy folio volumes with eye-strainingly small fonts.

However, the *Daodejing* has the advantages of being short, well-known, easily adapted to countercultural movements, and lacking the theological complexities of later Daoist movements. Probably for this reason I've come back to it again and again, to repair myself even if I can't repair the world.

13

In her classic short story "The Ones Who Walk Away from Omelas," Ursula K. Le Guin describes a utopian city, perfectly arranged to create lasting peace and happiness for its residents, and existing as an ongoing beacon of culture and civilization. The one and only cost to this utopia: it was founded upon the eternal torture of a single child, locked in darkness and dirt, in a basement. Le Guin is crystal-clear in her world-building that the basic premise is fixed and solid: for whatever undisclosed reason, there is no getting around the requirement to torture the child, and the situation cannot be changed. Confronted with the full facts of this inalterable situation, most residents acclimate themselves to the injustice of Omelas and make the most of it by going on to live their best lives.

Some do not: they are the ones who walk away, to somewhere we do not know, somewhere they do not know.

In the preface to a reprint edition, Le Guin describes interactions with readers angry with the ones who walk away and angry at her, as the author, for letting them walk away. They want the citizens of Omelas to stay and fight, to overturn the system—despite the clear ground rules for that fantasy world that overturning the system is not possible. These readers do not believe or do not accept the ground rules of that reality: perhaps the rules are a form of false consciousness imposed by Le Guin in her dastardly attempt to keep that poor fictional child in eternal torment. That is, after all, what "they" always want you to believe: that things are the way they are, and change is not possible.

That is, in fact, not what "they" always want you to believe. As a general rule, dictators do not want to preserve society untouched: most of the worst of them want to remake society. Did Hitler, Stalin, Mao, and Pol Pot try to preserve their nations the way they found them? Are Putin, Orbán, Erdoğan, Maduro, and Trump famous guardians of their nations' settled constitutional orders? What the worst "theys" want us to believe is that massive, overwhelming change is not only possible but urgent, demanded by nebulous threats.

Across all her work, Le Guin does not describe worlds in which social change is always impossible or a bad idea—for example, in *The Dispossessed* she proposes a qualified anarchistic utopia. But getting from real societies to utopias in her work is sometimes impossible, and often a bad idea. Sometimes, her characters are only allowed control over their own lives in the face of injustice—a control that the Ones Who Walk Away choose to exercise. This is consistent with the well-known and deep influence of the *Daodejing* on Le Guin's outlook: her characters often try to restrain their own interference in the world.

Le Guin was not a Sinologist, and her understandings of the *Daodejing*, frequently beautiful and stirring, are also heavily filtered through the lens of 1960s and 1970s Western countercultures. But her vision of walking away from injustice rather than fighting it is deeply resonant with ancient Chinese thought—both Confucianism and Daoism. Leaving is one of the most passive and most effective ways to fight fascism. One does not have to imagine a world in which Omelas is completely depopulated for justice to increase. This is what refugee communities have been doing for millennia: by fleeing an unjust state, they withdraw their capital, talents, and cultural wealth from polities that do not deserve them and carry them to ones that do. Refugee life can be devastating and tenuous, but refugee movements preserve more than they destroy and put inexorable pressure on the places they leave behind.

"America: love it or leave it!" was always good advice.

14

I know of exactly one social movement that has tried to incorporate Daoist walking away as a protest tactic.

The 2019 Hong Kong protests, which grew out of opposition to a law allowing extradition to mainland China, adopted the slogan, "Be Water." Rather than create a centralized structure with easily arrested leaders, protestors used "Be Water" to describe a way of organizing online in decentralized, leaderless fashion. It also applied to street tactics: flash mobs could quickly assemble to demonstrate; then, as soon as riot police arrived, they would melt away and reconnect somewhere else in the city.

The phrase was taken from Bruce Lee, who said, in a 1971 interview, "Empty your minds, be formless, shapeless, like water. Now you put water into a cup; it becomes the cup. You put it into a bottle; it becomes the bottle. You put it in a teapot; it becomes the teapot. Water can flow, or it can crash. Be water, my friends." This language of Lee's, however, was indebted to the *Daodejing*, which repeatedly describes the power and efficacy of water as a model for human behavior. It certainly made Lee's martial arts style, Jeet Kune Do, a flexible and beautiful holistic practice; and it seems to have added to the tactical success and longevity of the 2019 protests.

Unfortunately, the fact that the admonition to be water came through Lee's martial arts context may have framed it in the context of battle and limited the protestors in developing a larger strategic vision. No possible set of actions by the protestors could have caused the Communist Party to accede to democratic reforms in Hong Kong. They could have consolidated small concessions offered by the city's chief executive by melting away like water and kept more space for future protests on the table. Instead, a violent faction started beating police, erecting barricades, setting fires—guaranteeing a much harsher crackdown and many more long prison sentences. This was not the withdrawal of Ones Who Walk Away but of Ones Who Circle Around in a Flanking Movement.

The true way of water must be strategic, not just tactical: flowing from the deepest core of protestors' sense of self to their ultimate goals and melting away from conflict at every turn.

15

Strategic withdrawal from society is written all over the various strands of classical Daoist texts, but it does not belong to Daoism or to China. Withdrawal is a strategy that is continuously rediscovered, by individuals and by masses, across cultures and eras. Even when it is made only as an individual choice, with no intention to change society, it can change society. Think about Timothy Leary's admonition to "Turn on, tune in, drop out," and the rise of 1960s hippie counterculture—a truly marginal, short-lived movement that also changed American culture in lasting ways.

More recently, we discovered withdrawal again in a different form. During the middle of the pandemic, employees across

America started quitting their jobs, resulting in what was quickly dubbed the "Great Resignation." Employer demands on workers grew more severe at a time when many jobs had become actively dangerous to workers' health; faced with dire stakes in both isolation and in exposure, humans remembered that they were humans, not human resources. Even those who did not quit often engaged in "quiet quitting," doing the minimum possible labor to remain employed while disengaging their mental energy and their emotions from the workplace. As a result of the large-scale withdrawal of effective labor from the American economy, suddenly the United States had a labor shortage, and wages jumped. No amount of effort ever put into a campaign to raise a state or federal minimum wage had ever created as much additional income for American labor as did the simple collective choice of millions to withdraw.

In recent years, China has seen a similar but broader-based social movement of mass withdrawal, called "lying flat" or *tangping*. This was supercharged by the pandemic, but its roots are deeper: an earlier era of mass expansion of the Chinese university system had resulted in far more university graduates than the labor economy required. As a result, competition for entry-level white-collar jobs became impossibly cutthroat. Those who won the few spots available discovered that they had pawned their whole being to their managers: a seventy-two-hour workweek was well on the way to becoming fully normalized.

This situation of unsustainable levels of labor effort devoted solely to get ahead in a fruitless competition for diminishing resources was labeled "involution" or *neijuan*, a term borrowed from American social sciences research. As soon as the term was popularized online, it was applied broadly to many aspects of Chinese society: not just postcollegiate employment, but also the brutal college entrance-exam system and cutthroat competition between businesses across sectors. Corporations do not have the option to withdraw from society and lie flat, nor do most high-school seniors preparing for exams (stereotypical parents would hound them unceasingly if they tried). But college grads do, and they are.

An epidemic of lying flat will not end authoritarian rule in China any more than street protests did. *Tangping* seems to have confused policymakers in the central government, so there is no coherent response, but the government of the People's Republic of China is arguably the most stable in the world, and it is not going to suddenly dissolve. It is too soon to know how this recovery of the art of withdrawal will change China, and researchers are only beginning to publish on the phenomenon. Anecdotal evidence suggests that an enormous development of cultural capacity is happening as people turn to the arts and to online content creation, to reading, and to volunteer work. After the Mongol conquest of China, the temporary end of the bureaucratic exam system sent thousands of well-educated literati out into the world to make a living from their books; they ended up creating Chinese drama and vernacular fiction. We do not know yet what the lying-flat generation will create, but it will likely be stunning—how could tens of millions of highly educated, plugged-in creative people in their twenties with lots of time not do something that will change the world?

16

Lying flat won't cause sudden democratization of China or America, but that doesn't mean it isn't useful for achieving social change. Nor is its effectiveness limited to the chance alignment of choices among uncoordinated masses. Withdrawal from participation in society, one of the quintessential hallmarks of Daoist practice, is also a strategy usable by organizations and individuals with clear reformist goals in mind.

A strike is a withdrawal. This is hard to see: the word "strike" itself is a word of force, and strikes are usually carried out with a show of force. Marching, chanting, waving placards, campaigning and union drives, and belligerent speeches to the media by union leaders are the images we associate with strikes. But at its heart, any strike is a withdrawal of labor from the employer—a negative act. It is in the withdrawal that the strike has its force: the employer becomes unable to deliver on its contracts with customers. The spectacle put on for cameras is not where the leverage lies—and in many cases a strike probably could succeed more quickly without it.

Anything else called a "strike" works in the same way, applying pressure through withdrawal: rent strikes, tuition strikes, sex strikes. Any kind of boycott is the same: a withdrawal of commerce from an offending vendor. Draft evasion is a form of withdrawal rarely centrally coordinated, but it regularly becomes a social movement during unpopular wars; if widespread enough, it can meaningfully impair a military's ability to fight. Any and all strikes can be and are combined with media and public spectacle, but the leverage is not in the visible activity. The leverage is in the empty space of the withdrawal—as the *Daodejing* puts it, "Thirty spokes share one hub; it is in that emptiness that the cart has use."

Does the accompanying angry pageantry have use? It can. Situations exist in which the leverage is unusually poor, the institution unusually susceptible to public opinion, and public opinion unusually sympathetic to activists. When meeting such conditions, then the decorations for the withdrawal can be needed to maximize effect. No algorithm can measure the exact balances for when it is time to bring out the placards or put them back in the storage unit. One must look at the full reality of how things are and judge a way through without a rule.

Most organizers do use a rule: spectacle, every time, the busier the better. The withdrawal is nothing in itself; it is a zero and an absence. It is only a platform upon which the show can be run, and the show must run, panting, to the end. It is hard to imagine strikes, boycotts, or draft evasion as just a retreat and a nonparticipation, because the media-mediated is what has always seemed to count. In fact, it is just a simulacrum of action: the real action is in the nonaction of disengagement, where the leverage lies working. To forget this is to create diversions, backlash, side debates, troll bait, blame games, and media criticism.

To keep a focus on the real fulcrum of action, one must clear one's head of all the inspiring visuals that serve as a sign for and replacement of what works.

17

Inspiration is a terrible thing, seizing the mind with an ideological buzz. Inspiration leads away from clear thought and toward bad choices. Inspiration leads to mass death.

Hong Kong is the one place, more than any other, that has kept alive the memory of the Tiananmen protests. From 1990 through 2019, candlelight vigils were held every year on the anniversary of June 4. Internet freedom has been much more open than in mainland China, and full histories of what happened at Tiananmen were always available. Many of the 2019 protestors (and those in the earlier 2014 umbrella movement) took inspiration from Tiananmen. It didn't help; it hastened the closure of Hong Kong's freedoms.

Or again, the Arab Spring started in Tunisia and succeeded in Tunisia. And then it caused civil war in Libya, civil war in Syria, civil war in Yemen, replacement of one Egyptian autocrat by another (with a brief electoral interlude), and more garden-variety repressions in Morocco and Saudi Arabia. The United Nations' estimates of the Yemeni civil war death toll had reached 377,000 by the end of 2021; 2024 estimates of the Syrian civil war death toll stood at almost 618,000.

When I watched the Hong Kong protests on television, I could not watch them the same way, as a teenager, that I had watched Tiananmen unfold. I followed them obsessively but with less wonder and less thrill. Some of my academic colleagues in China studies posted statements about hope and inspiration, but I don't think anyone was naive about where it was likely to lead. I could understand the inspiration, but I couldn't feel more than an echo of it. I felt the dread one feels when hearing the words "Don't go in there" spoken in a horror movie. Like a well-trained audience member, I knew exactly what would happen next, and I had to watch the genre-blind characters play out their roles toward ruin.

18

At the same time as pro-Palestine protests took over the world's headlines in 2023–2024, Canada saw a much smaller and very different protest movement bubble up on the populist right. The "Axe the Tax" movement fought the Trudeau government's carbon tax; it received significant attention and boosting from the national Conservative Party leader, as well as from conservative provincial premiers.

The Axe the Tax movement broke all the rules: it was a mess of a protest movement. It showed no sign of organization or coordination. It had no message discipline: antitax messages were mixed in with conspiracy theories about vaccines and world government—and even flat-earth insanity. No one had any media training. People were posting anything and everything to random antitax Facebook pages that seem to come and go. And it wasn't very large: it may have had as few as a hundred core protestors nationwide.

In Alberta, the conservative western province where I live, the primary protest venue was in a rest stop along Route 2, near the small prairie town of Lacombe. Perhaps a dozen protestors lived for a few months in campers parked off the rest stop. They had a kids' area and a welcome tent where they offered free coffee and food to anyone who wanted to come in. They had some flags and signs up, but they usually didn't march anywhere, give speeches, chant, or wave placards. They just hung out at the rest stop and talked to people. Probably the custom-painted "Axe the Tax" tractor trailer parked by the encampment was a gift of the oil companies that would have benefited from their work, but otherwise there was little sign of corporate funding or efficiency that one might associate with a rightist astroturf operation.

As few and strange as they were, the Axe the Tax protestors seemed at the time much more likely to win their fight than the on-campus pro-Palestine movement. Why?

- *They were demanding exactly what they wanted.* They wanted to axe the tax, and they demanded that the tax be axed. Campus protestors wanted Palestine to be liberated, and they demanded that universities make small changes to their investment portfolios.
- *They addressed the polities who could make change.* They were talking to Canadians, who are the ones who vote for the Canadian Parliament. Campus protestors were talking to everyone except the Israelis who vote for the Israeli Knesset.
- *They were nudging people who were already sympathetic.* Their rest-stop home base was in a conservative-friendly rural area. They were talking to motorists who were spending a lot on gasoline, pushing them very gently toward signing a petition and showing up to vote. Campus protestors, in pursuit of their minimalist demands, shouted maximalist slogans at a mixed, often skeptical audience.
- *They had close ties to allied politicians.* National and provincial conservative leaders and their staff visited the protestors and largely earned their support. Campus protestors in most countries considered it a badge of honor to trash their

respective left-center parties and wouldn't meet with any but the farthest left.

- *They self-marginalized.* The Alberta Axe the Tax group took up half of a rest stop: a literally and figuratively marginal space. They didn't bother anyone who didn't seek them out. In contrast, pro-Palestinian protestors sat across major bridges and airport toll roads, deliberately causing long, alienating delays.

- *They welcomed.* Right-wing populists are often weird and frightening—for example, in Charlottesville in 2017, or at the Capitol on January 6; but the Axe the Tax group at least tried to be friendly, inviting people in for coffee or a meal. Highway signs by the turnoff advertised free hugs. This is not inherently alienating to people who aren't read into the issue. On the other hand, campus protestors celebrated Hamas, demanded more anticolonial violence, masked their faces, and insisted on using slogans that they knew were received badly. All of this is alienating to those who aren't read in.

- *They were quiet.* Half-hour rambling rants posted to Facebook aren't everyone's favorite, but they don't replicate the experience of being shouted at by a crowd. In their own encampment the protestors didn't do much shouting at all; mostly they just had conversations with visitors. Sometimes they listened to visitors' stories of their traumas and had a cry with them. No megaphones or microphones were to be seen.

There are very serious limits to how wonderfully harmonious this movement was. It included nonwhite participants, and one of the leaders at the Alberta rest stop was a Cree woman; but in other places around the encampment, one could find racist, dog-whistle graffiti. And explicitly homophobic and transphobic rants were posted to Facebook—I would have been very worried for any trans men or women who decided to stop in for a visit with them. Much was terrible about this movement, but it won. Mark Carney barely led the Liberals to an election victory in April, but he did so while promising to axe the tax. His campaign website put it this way: "The Consumer Carbon Tax isn't working—it's become too divisive. That's why I'll cancel it and replace it with incentives to reward people for greener choices." Weird, friendly, loopy, sympathetic far-right grannies sitting on the roadside were not the ones who got called divisive; their mostly polite opposition caused the Liberal party to call its own policy divisive and set it on the road to repeal.

The Axe the Tax movement, a few dozen people who had gone down the rabbit hole of right-populism, forced a retreat from the man who had served as the governor of both the Bank of Canada and the Bank of England. The reason? Without knowing a thing about Laozi, the movement had mastered his advice: understanding the ultimate goals, prioritizing harmony over conflict, not bothering with efficient and clever planning, retreating from language toward silence, minimizing the scope of their interventions in society, pushing along with the flow rather than against it, abandoning themselves to spontaneity and naturalness.

It is a terrible irony that mimicry of nature put the axe to nature's root.

19

Grand, world-historical mobilizations can thud, dumbly.

Lying flat can sweep away injustice, as the fascists flail.

Do nothing, and there is nothing you do not do.

The stakes of fighting Trump are higher than the stakes of Canadian environmental policy: the American democratic order hangs in the balance. However, the potential end of self-governance does not mean that we should fight harder than ever before, with bigger protests, noisier chants, better-coordinated social media, and more disruptive subversions of the normal order of American life. Instead, it requires us to calibrate both our actions and our nonactions as finely as we can to produce the best outcomes available while rigorously denying ourselves the psychic pleasures of confrontation whenever it would be counterproductive.

Trump owns the phantasmagoric circus. He's the mirage-making midway barker; the fecal flimflam flinger; the crassest, classless Gatsby; the Great American Con Man. He's the choreographer for all the bedazzled brouhahas in the Wrestlemania of the Public Id. A good general never accepts an invitation to fight on the enemy's preferred ground, and a smart activist will not want to jump into Trump's ring. Any action that is about spectacle, presence, airtime, or virality is a show for that ring: it does not raise consciousness, it does not reach new ears, it does not persuade. These are just grand mal quote retweets. They platform while they perform and create new theaters for backlash.

Americans seem to have intuited this, without consensus or consistency. The massive Women's March at Trump's first inaugural was the largest protest event in the history of the United States, and it had no noticeable effect on how Trump's first term played out: he went on to appoint the justices who overturned *Roe v. Wade*. As a result, the People's March at the second inaugural was much smaller, only about a tenth the size. That makes sense: everyone had had a crystal-clear demonstration that the first inaugural protest was useless.

And yet I am writing this one week after the Hands Off! protests, the first mass-mobilization event of Trump's second term. It got plenty of media coverage! There were many posts about it! But there is no evidence that it has resulted in a shift in tactics from Democratic lawmakers, much less backtracking from Trump or his Republican allies. Those who argue for the effectiveness of protests often point to social science research showing that issue-specific protests in response to damaging Trump policies meaningfully move public opinion, but three problems come with applying this research to the promotion of mass rallies.

- First, this research has a hard time disentangling reaction against the offending policies themselves, from reaction in favor of the protests against the offending policies—in many cases, there is no good reason to think that public opinion might not have moved against a policy if it caused no protests.
- Second, small, issue-focused protests directed against local authorities responsive to the grassroots are not the same as large, coalitional, multi-issue nationwide actions directed at a highly insulated president.
- And finally, public opinion in itself does not matter unless it can be made effective through functioning democratic elections or other directly effective civil-society actions.

In the week following the Hands Off! protests, Trump's massive tariffs placed on the entire world caused a near stock-market crash, expectations of massive layoffs, and promises of renewed, supercharged inflation. Trump's actions, not activist counteractions, caused a sudden massive drop in his popularity. The only thing necessary is to lie flat on one's back and get out of his way while he ruins his own coalition.

20

For the first year of the war in Gaza, I did not eat well, and I stopped exercising. I couldn't sleep. I found it a terrible effort to shower and often did not. I upped my dosage of Celexa.

Sometimes, for the sake of my health, my wife cajoled me into taking walks in Edmonton's river valley. I do not see Nature like one of the British Romantics, as a sympathetic and symbolic reflection of my mind. That was probably for the best, the way my mind ran those days. What I could accept, because it is all I can ever find when I visit, was the alienness of the woods. Things move very slightly around my peripheral vision. The treetops have some breeze motion. Something cracks a twig. Far into the brush, perhaps an owlet's head makes a tiny swivel. These things have their own patterns of motion and tracks of being; they do not run according to the very narrow courses that I can set myself, locked in the desk drawers of the administrative state. They are also not about words. Since the stresses of that year, I found myself hating words as well. Perhaps what we need is a genocide of words.

Taking oneself out of the world isn't usually a good option. But sometimes in the woods, I started to think that I'd like to take myself out of myself.

21

Under the care of a doctor and a therapist, I learned how to loosen the knots in my endocrine system that had been tied by threat. Fewer starches and more greens. More varied and better-timed workouts. Sleep hygiene. No news after noon. Doomscrolling never. Daily mindfulness practice. Reading high and low. Sunlight.

I also rediscovered what it was in the vastly varied texts of Daoism that had drawn my interest, before I was capable of the scholarly delineations of stream from stream that grounded origins in the variegated bubbling of Warring States China's soup. I am done being a convert, and there's nothing in Daoism's origins to convert to, just a series of habits that add up to a power of vision. I returned to my favorite texts and began to practice that power again. Starting to look again, and again harder, at the natural world and the social, I could see the isolinear diagrams that ran through things, measuring out their weak and hard. I remembered that the world has a grain like the grain of sliced meat: utterly impossible to render in words and just as impossible not to see if you know how to look.

Having reset myself, I was able to read the news of election results with equanimity. It was easier for me to do so than others: I don't even live in the United States anymore, and I wouldn't be particularly under threat if I did. But I was reassured to see online a large number of marginalized and threatened voices that knew the same secrets of resiliency that I had rediscovered through study and practice. There was mass despair but also less-mass balance and strength.

The world continues. Good can be done. Good can happen, spontaneously, by doing nothing. Other good can happen by doing many things that do not prioritize conflict. This is not a matter of hope. Hope and despair depart equally from the true landforms of the world, a map of bumpy rutted and elevated possibility. It is a matter of looking out over that possibility and picking out one's course step-by-step.

22

In her award-winning book *Care Activism*, Professor Ethel Tungohan describes a variety of ways in which migrant care workers provide support and care to each other in their activism as a natural outgrowth of their labor. Alongside many "normal" and sometimes-effective versions of activism, including strikes and street protests by and for migrant caregivers, she also describes a Filipina beauty pageant, Miss Caregiver, held every year by relatively conservative migrant-advocacy organizations in Ontario. Beauty pageants are not legendary for being at the cutting edge of liberationist movements. Their explicit politics are usually nil, and their contextualization in terms of traditional gender roles usually pegs them as solidly regressive. Yet the nonthreatening nature of the events gave them deep resources for advocacy with the regressive Harper government:

> *When the Conservative government was in power in Canada, the Fil-Core Support Group was able to award the winner of the beauty pageant a trip to Ottawa, where they got a personal tour of the House of Commons and a one-on-one meeting with former immigration minister Jason Kenney, during which they had the opportunity to discuss issues facing migrant domestic workers. For instance, one of the judges for the 2017 beauty pageant was Miss Caregiver 2010, who used her platform to campaign to clear the backlog in permanent residency applications. (185)*

When the same Jason Kenney ran for premier of Alberta (Canada's most conservative province), he included in his platform a promise to *increase* the number of immigrants to Alberta's ultraconservative rural communities by ten thousand annually. And after his win, Alberta indeed saw a huge spike in immigration, including thousands of Filipina care workers. That did not happen because of a single beauty pageant in Ontario, nor did Alberta become a paradise for migrant labor. However, that one historical track underscores the importance of gentle, friendly pushes from groups perceived to be either allies or at least nonhostile. One reason that Canadian conservatism is so much less xenophobic than American conservatism is the greater tendency of many Canadian first-generation immigrants to become actively involved with the Conservative party.

When one is already on the inside, able to meet with decision-makers and have a friendly, detailed conversation, there's no need to take to the streets. Why do we spend so much time, effort, and money on being the fiercest possible enemies to our enemies, when we could instead disarm them with vulnerability and talk to them? This doesn't always work, but it fails much less often than shouting.

23

The hot new fad is *dark woke*: going full dirtbag for a glorious tomorrow.

The idea is: the right started in with the insults and the violence, and they've earned payback. When they go low, we go high explosive. Being beige and reasonably bow-tied against their vomit tsunami got us more Trump. So, let the fuck loose.

This was predictable under the fundamental laws of psychohistory: losers radicalize. Then they lose harder. Group dynamics of the out-group will always push toward extremism and away from mirrors. But how does one explain this to people wrapped up in glory and ire?

Credit (for the sake of argument) that the Opponents are indeed not human. Grant that they are Lovecraftian bubbling piles of slithering tentacles, all eyes and horror and orifices. Allow that what they deserve and require is the Full Dalek: exterminate, exterminate, straight from the toilet plunger.

Still: What works? And what are your options?

Soaring Obaman light and goodness that embraces all humanity within its wings is not the only alternative to the dark woke. You do not have to believe that if one persists in sainthood that one day, at the second coming of Karl Marx, all the nasty Magas will realize that you were nice and pretty all along. Truly, they won't.

Without that naiveté, one can still shed the dark woke and wear the gray wooze. The gray wooze does not hope for sweetness and light. The gray wooze does not destroy and it does not convert; it evades. Not needing to fight or to forgive, the gray wooze becomes a muffling nothing that sucks the energy out of aggression and leaves the opponent still angry but confused and listless.

Decrease salience. Stream something else. Go gray wooze.

24

The quieter and more confusing the activism, the smaller its scale and the worse its alignment with battle lines—indeed, the closer to being nothing at all that it becomes—the more assuredly it will have an effect.

There is nothing particularly dramatic about a Filipina beauty queen getting a sit-down with the Canadian minister of immigration—it doesn't play out on the evening news. But it is more substantive in forcing the minister to hear, and to respond, than a slogan on a placard. Why is the U.S. Congress so constantly eager to represent the interests of wealthy donors? Because their money is needed for campaigns, but also because the money buys access and creates relationships: when representatives live in a constant swirl of backslapping steak dinners and rounds of self-satisfied golf, the money and the political interests and the friendly relations will merge into interwoven strands of the same very tight ligatures. Elon Musk did not catch Trump's attention by standing outside Mar-a-Lago with a bullhorn.

Few have the scratch to get a sit-down with a president. Quite a few can cut a check to get the same with a member of the House of Representatives. Pretty much anyone can get a completely free meeting with a town councilor just by asking for one. Polite, sustained, substantial engagement will almost always be more effective than external pressure. Would you rather be in the room where it happens or in a designated protest area across the street from the complex that includes the building housing the room where it happens?

For most of us, that kind of effect is only possible with locally centered activism. That means giving up on the false hope that one can meaningfully fight off the world-historical injustice. But it is healthful to give up on that hope. International headlines are the realm of grand-scale spectacle, the outrage carnival, the phantasm. The local is where everyone lives—most of all, those living in war zones. It is not a failure of allyship to do nothing for the far off, when no action one could take would help them and some might hurt. There is no ethical obligation to perform a pantomime of saving others for an audience of oneself.

Most of the world's great religions emphasize the importance of small acts of service while relieving individual believers of the responsibility to save the world. This is where all of us end up, anyway: we do not save the world, and cannot. Guilting ourselves into trying is useless at best, dangerous to ourselves and others at worst.

25

A few definitions of "to lie," as adapted from the *Borgesian Dictionary of English* (1978 edition):

- to be prone
- to be horizontally extended
- to be abed
- to be dead
- to speak or write statements that are not strictly true
- (biblically) to propagate the species; to smash and/or bump uglies
- to remain indefinitely in a subject position while exposed to any kind of degrading treatment, torture, or simple imprisonment
- to persist in a state of concealment, usually in the bushes
- to utter utter falsehood
- to prepare to entrap
- to squat behind that corner, hand on sword pommel
- to sojourn as a guest in the land
- to pitch a military camp

- to live under unspecified circumstances
- to be foisted upon, as with a city garrison
- (with gerund) to keep on keepin' on
- to be placed in a position with a shorter z-axis than x-axis or y-axis
- to rest
- to be; alternatively, not to be
- (of ships) to be anchored at a port
- to play dirty against a competitor
- to be legally admissible
- To think of England
- to tell fables or amusing anecdotes
- to pickle in lye; to prepare lutefisk

An order of things is reflected in language. This is not determinative (the structure of language is not a prison house) but an order of the possibilities upon which language opens. That is because words accrete the experiences and the psychic connections of people over time, conjoining them into various possibilities of meaning. Some senior professors of literature seize on this polysemy to track the possible divergences of a text into different interpretive routes: a single variant reading of a line can send the entire textual contraption off in an unexpected direction. Nevertheless, that process can be run in reverse: one can trace back divergent meanings across the course of historical etymologies to where they all conjoin.

Lying flat is the ultimate passive action, a mere taking up of space, a mimicry of death. But it is in its passivity that it becomes the repository of action: one lies with, in sex, and creates life. One lies in wait, in war, and brings death. Lying through one's teeth has a different etymology, but their distinct Old Germanic parents converged fortuitously into a single English word. Lying flat is not what it seems. Lying lies. It projects complete submission while it masters from below.

26

Today I am lying on the slowly regreening grass in a power line cut, accepting nature as it comes and waiting.

Below me, to the east, the land slopes down into the Whitemud Creek ravine, then back up the other side, far off toward the warehouse district and the rail connections. The catenaries loping above me say nothing—because it is a sunny day, they can carry their freight of electrons in silence. It is only during light mists of rain or snow that one can hear them crackling off the moisture. Down here on the ground, there are only breeze, earthly smells, and a pair of magpies pecking at something in the grass. A cyclist or a dog walker passes by on the path every few minutes. The cut is lined on either side by tract housing—not nearly as extravagant as the weekend villas that now fill my old haunts in exurban Beijing, and not nearly thick enough to keep out subjection to accident but playing their own role in a balanced urban order.

Elsewhere, the normally terrible things happen. Illegal deportations of Venezuelan migrants and Palestinian students continue. Homelessness is spiking in Moncton. J. D. Vance mocks China as a nation of peasants. Russia bombs civilians in Ukraine yet again. Orbán has declared all Hungarians male or female. Health care has been defunded for a single autistic Ojibwe girl in Thunder Bay. Thirteen million Sudanese humans have fled genocide.

I can and have donated, posted, signed petitions, called politicians, and even marched in the street. I will do so again. But the terrible things remain out of my hands. I will not make them worse or better. Most of what I have done for others I have done for myself, not for others, fighting off survivor's guilt rather than oppressors.

That which I can do for real, to tip things toward the better, I can do without thinking of myself or the world. When a hammer lies at hand, one grasps it. Endless conference rooms and Zoom meetings are the place where, with an ignoble but caffeinated spirit, I can push for one obstacle to be removed or one person to be included. Those are the pressure points in front of me, and I press on them. Mastery of the world is not a divine power over history. Mastery of the world is knowing the technique to polish it, very finely, to a shine.

Lying here, prone, back to the grass and chest out to the universe, I am purposefully ridiculous. No Atlas, I do not carry the world on my shoulders and do not go wandering space. Still, no ordinate system outside of perspective can fix me. I am lying in a gash in nature cut by industry, or I am lying in an industrial space recolonized by nature. I am down or up, I am supine or I am at the front. Knowing the rotation of these binaries, knowing exactly how I look, I can visit the truth beyond either and or. Being only what I am, no victim to despair or to hope, I am free to move forward on my back.

The Activist

Saying

1

WHAT IS SHOUTED IS NOT WHAT IS THOUGHT. WHAT IS HOWLED is not what gave birth to the heart. The trace before the thought is the beginning of justice, and the parent of the heart is the origin of every movement.

You must pull back from your own words to return to that origin, before you launch again into speech. Then you can know speech and its millionfold ends.

Back and forth, the journey of the Activist, from end to source to end: because there is no end of ends, no source for the source, there can be no success unless one is motionless in every fist pump.

2

There is what is said, and then there is the language in which it is said. The language is a prison that puts everything said into its place. The words can wriggle, but they cannot wriggle free from their cells.

That structure that captures what is said is not the structure of society, nor is it the structure of nature. Those have their own languages, which are not yours. To confuse what you say at a protest for the fact of the world is a constant danger: your own words lead you on, away from your goal and into a structure where you cannot effect change. Self-imprisonment within slogans is not the route to liberation.

Therefore, the Activist sees through words to the reality beyond, sees through the reality to the emptiness. They are familiar with words but remain aloof from them, like meeting someone distasteful at a party.

3

The world names the lifeless, A Towering Marble. The world names the cruel, A Whirlwind of Poppies. But Death and Life give birth to each other, Starvation and Plenitude feed each other, Hatred and Love embrace each other, Injustice and Justice license each other, Misery and Joy complete each other, War and Peace are at concord with each other.

Therefore, do not bask in the right and think that by the right you will make all right; because the right is what creates wrong, and there is no wrong that did not suckle from right. The Activist fights for the right to evaporate right and wrong.

Beyond the opposites is the place of achievement: working forever because nothing can be won.

4

Every word has its antonym: you cannot use one without summoning the ghost of the other.

Most people have never learned the trick of seeing through words; for them, the word brings along the reality. Therefore, when you use a word in a protest, most people will not see the hint of a ghost but feel the claws of a monster. This is the only way that words can work: there is never light without equal darkness, and the flash creates the shadow.

The simpler and louder your shouts of hope, the starker and more ravenous the despair will appear. Therefore, pull back on your words, make them soft as stockings on a palace stair. Hold them in and twist them up in looping knots of qualifications, and the sources of fear will also appear to be bound and gagged. You will not frighten away a crowd, but you will entice a gaggle.

5

There isn't much divergence between yes and no. There isn't much distance between true and false. These are words that point only at other words, and they do not ever have any point of contact with the world. Back and forth is the motion that gets you ever more stuck at the center of the web.

So, when everyone else is arguing, happy to hate, as if words are the spring warm sea sun, then shut yourself down and give no word at all. Be a blank newborn who cannot laugh. Everyone else retires to a decorated tent, so walk a ways off and lie face down on the dirt. Be sleepy, be stupid, be confused, and in the morning let the others shout and argue, chasing lap after lap.

You will be nourished by something that has no point of contact with words. You will roll up a frosted-over tarp and regret nothing but a past love.

6

The Activist takes only the course. The course is a thing topsy-turvy, so turvy and so topsy. Within that mess is an image, flummoxed. Behind the image is an object, blurred. In the organs of the object is the True Sperm, the germ of holding faith.

From the most ancient protests to the most modern, the Activist has learned to hold faith in that most inward and inexpressible recess of the course, not in the evident. The evident is where words waste away.

7

Holding faith is something taught by language but perfected outside of language. The possibility of holding faith is there in the word, which seems to gesture toward a thing. If the word and the thing match, this is coded "true." The word holds faith with the thing.

But there are no words for the thing that lies the deepest, at the ground of all being. One must learn to hold faith with that thing outside of language, by a practice outside of language.

Holding faith with the goal of the movement must also take place outside of language, if you have been wise enough to know that the true goal cannot fit within language.

8

Do not, under any circumstances, get your message out.

Hold that message in, like a great Peng bird inside its egg, and let it take ten thousand years to grow. Keep it there, encased in the hardest of shells and safe. Nestle it to incubate, never pressuring it. Have faith that it will hatch, though it will still be egg by the time your civilization has died, and the next civilization after that.

9

Words are without loyalties. The word you send will betray as soon as it leaves you, conveying the message that the listener wants to hear, not the message you entrusted to it.

The most faithless words are slogans angrily shouted by the group. These words are unconstrained, because they are so short and so few. They convey mainly threat, with no content: intelligible shrapnel.

The next-most faithless words are careful position statements offered as clips for television and social media by the designated spokesperson who has had media training. These are constrained only by audible bad faith. They convey a clear, overly simple position shot through with green schemes.

The next-most faithless words after that are open dialogues held at the margins of a large protest by people trusted to speak for themselves and with no cameras in sight. These are constrained in proportion to your calmness and purity of intention. They convey uninformed sincerity.

The next-most faithless words after that are conversations held behind closed doors in meetings with administrators. These are constrained by full contextualization with opportunities to explain, PowerPoints of data tables, and a calm, professional demeanor. They convey well-informed desire for collaborative problem-solving.

The only faithful words are those not spoken, as one sits with a friend or an enemy in silence and touches their arm in sympathy. These unspoken words convey the entire truth of the world and of your being in it.

10

The softest thing in the world can trample the hardest thing in the world. Something with no existence can fit in a region of no dimension.

That is why I know the boon of nonaction and the efficacy of communicating without words.

Almost no one understands this, and that ignorance doubles its power.

11

It is only when the best course goes unused that people can coin the phrase "collective action." It is only because of common cowardice that one can see "courage." It is only when people please themselves that one can laud "self-sacrifice." It is only when there is no sense of future that one can admire "hope."

These are not virtues; they are words and symptoms.

12

Positive words for yourself are as dangerous as negative words for the other. Do not hold your value words tightly in your mind: these are swamp-gas demons, and they will lead you like the will-o'-the-wisp into the mire. Remember that every word that describes a goodness was born with an evil twin. If you make the one real in your head, the other will burrow into your spleen.

Better to see through them both as illusory, because they are both illusory. Then you will be liberated to act toward the goal in the most effective way possible, without being diverted by your sense of self.

Beleaguered by negation and despair, show no affirming flame.

13

The knower does not speak, and the speaker does not know.

Bolt the doors, fasten the windows, dull the knife, loosen the knots, dim the bulbs: this is the Obscure Unity in which all things melt in shadow.

This wordless state cannot be touched by near or far, help or harm, priceless or cheap, and so it is priceless.

14

To know the use of words, one must plant a root firmly in what has no words. By planting a root in what has no words, one can draw one's sustenance from what is better than words. By drawing one's sustenance from what is better than words, one will not rely upon words. By not relying upon words, one can use words only when and how they advance one to the goal.

The place beyond words where one plants the root is called the course. The course is always empty of traffic, so the root of the self will always be safe there.

15

There is a good silence and a bad silence.

The good silence is the silence of the Activist. The Activist does not shout slogans and does not lead chants. They do not give speeches, and they do not go on television for interviews. Instead, they sit with people, one at a time, and do not say much. Perhaps they whisper something in an ear. They have a conversation, but it is short. And so the Activist is seen as the carrier of a secret, important and nonthreatening.

The bad silence is the silence of the follower. The follower repeats a shouted mantra: "Do not engage!" at anyone who wants to have a dialogue. The follower repeats to the reporters, "I am not authorized to talk to you" and directs them to the one who is slick and media trained. So the followers are put on YouTube as speechless, mindless cogs in a protest machine who do not know why they are there and who defer always to the truth of the great leader. This is called "gagging the tools."

16

Trustworthy language is not catchy, and catchy language is not trustworthy. The good do not debate online, and online debaters are up to no good. Those who understand are not those with the PhDs, and those with the PhDs do not understand.

This is why the Activist does not pile up anything: neither respect, nor self-respect, nor power. The more they do for others, the more they do for themself. The more they give to others, the more they have for themself.

The course of the universe is to bring without taking. The course of the Activist is to do without struggle.

17

Why do I only use words to say that words should not be used? You only see the words that I use; you cannot see the words that I do not use.

Why do I use words at all? Why do I not retreat into the wordlessness of peach and plum trees, heaped upon the spring? Because I am only a human; I am not the Activist. The Activist has never once spoken, and yet they called into being the framework of time and space. The Activist has never once written, and yet they have already narrated the annals of all that is past, or passing, or to come.

I can only make half-hearted attempts to shed myself of words, I cannot be palpable and mute. Some stories need telling, even when they can't be told. There's a way to spit out the wordless words, but they sound like plucked notes circling in the wind and rain.

Nonetheless, given that the best words are not words, it's no surprise that these nostrums of mine are incredibly hard to get and harder to live out.

18

These nostrums of mine are incredibly easy to get and to live out. Yet no one in the whole world seems to get them or to live them out. Why not?

Words trace their descent to what lies behind signification, and acts have a ruler in the basic structure of time and space. People do not live in those places of what is hidden without a philosophical or spiritual practice; they get stuck on surfaces and hence only see and hear what they can see and hear. Therefore, those who can really understand me are few, and those who critique me are honored.

This is why the Activist keeps a metaphysical wad of cash zipped away safely under their rags.

Acting

1

DO NON-DOING, ACT NONACTION, TASTE THE TASTELESS. ENLARGE the small and increase the few, and you will be able to repay what is not deserved.

Thread your plans for the difficult through the cracks of the easy. Construct your massive home on the foundation of the small. Everything difficult is accomplished in the easy, everything massive is built upon the small. This is how the Activist is great, through lacking any greatness.

Hold faith with the cause by making no promises.

2

Do nothing, and nothing will remain undone.

This is not what most protestors want or understand. They have come out because something must be done. They are energized because they want to be the type of people who act. They prize the action over the goal. Even destroying the goal is an acceptable price to pay, as long as they have destroyed it with righteous intent.

The Activist is the one who knows not to act. They are a black hole, sitting motionless in the center of the galaxy, drawing in a hundred billion worlds without ever showing a sign.

3

They who can hold power back in their mouth are like sated infants mouthing the nipple: they do not need to act, they do not need to speak, and all threats are kept screened off, all nourishment supplied. They have not congealed into an upright body, they have not known division into genders, and yet, inchoate little chaoses, they rule all around.

Those who cannot hold anything back but put their power forth are like adults, angular and injured, acting in labor and losing their substance, earning a disgusting meal, scraping little bits of surplus that add up to nothing: this is the method of "Boxing Oxygen."

Therefore, the Activists hold back their power; and their goal is delivered to them.

4

There are two kinds of nonaction: the nonaction of the raw lumber, and the nonaction of water.

The course of the raw lumber is simpler. The only thing the block could do by moving is to topple over, and the only thing it could achieve by toppling over is to injure; therefore, it does nothing. In most situations that call forth activism, no action exists that will not make things worse. Do not assume that there must be a solution, or that there is a correct action that will fix the problem. See clearly, past your own words, to the true dynamics of the situation that lie beyond words. Understand your own power to injure and that you can never only injure your enemies. If only injury is possible, pull back before you have begun and be the raw lumber.

The course of water is more complex. Flowing water seems to carry a thought. It does much by moving: it wears down mountains and creates life. But water moves chaotically, in dynamically incalculable ways for which there are no words; and it always moves downward. In a few situations that call forth activism, there may be a watery action that will make things better—very slightly and very slowly. Water acts passively, drop by drop, and activism will be more effective the more it resembles the passivity of water: the march surpasses the uprising, the rally surpasses the march, the teach-in surpasses the rally, the sit-in surpasses the teach-in, and the sick-out surpasses the sit-in. This is how one achieves the power of water's action: moving ever downward, toward calmness, passivity, loneliness, and life.

5

When the course is every street in a city, people are at home, and the streets are empty. When the course is no street in a city, then the people take to the streets.

Marches are not good; they only mark the absence of good. It would be better if no one could think of any unmet needs: desire is a death wish.

The trick is learning how to die headfirst.

6

The smart person with power does not use their power, and that is why they have power. The dumb person with the power never stops using their power, and that is why they lose power. The smart person accomplishes everything by never using their power. The dumb person fails at everything by always using their power.

The person who models altruism does not know not to act, but at least they mean well. The person who models justice does not know not to act, and they are up to something. The person who models administrative procedure does not know how to act, and when their actions fail, they call in the cops.

Therefore, only when the course was lost did people need power. Only when correct use of power was forgotten did people need altruism. Only when altruism failed did people go toward justice. Only when justice lost its meaning was administrative procedure established. And then: the cops.

Branches bear buds, buds open into flowers, flowers give way to fruit. If you want your movement to bear fruit, wait and do nothing.

7

The supreme good is like water.

Water flows down to those who need it: an elk lowering its head to drink from the stream, silvergrass upon a lower western slope, a young girl who needs to wash the stink from her curls. Water never launches an uprising. It settles in calm, in the lowest of the low.

In a march, it is the road that matters. In a sit-in, it is the seat that matters. In an occupation, it is the building that matters. In a boycott, it is the unspent dollar that matters. In a placard, it is the handle that matters. In a slogan, it is the unvoiced intention that matters.

Change comes from the unmoved foundation: that which does not contend, does not engage, and does not act. Like water, the activist grounds themself in the lowest place and becomes still there.

8

The anus is a miraculous spout.

Detestable and ridiculous, dirty and beneath, it gives and does not tire. It fertilizes. It puts life through all its transformations.

Hold onto the spirit of the anus, because the Activist is a miraculous spout, detestable and ridiculous, dirty and beneath.

9

Respect and disrespect are equal dangers in group dynamics.

If one has respect, one will fear losing respect. If one receives disrespect, one will thirst for respect.

The way to earn respect, and to wash away disrespect, is always to take one more step toward militancy than the current equilibrium point. Step-by-step, driven by their own taste for affirmation, all the members of the protest will jointly steer their movement into blindness and disaster.

If you care about the goal, empty yourself of the need to be respected. Be despised by your peers, be the sellout, and win.

10

Crookedly complete, bently straight, emptily full, oldly new, lackingly sated, and plentifully confused: this is how the Activist hugs tight to Oneness and becomes a model for the movement.

They do not show off and so become famous. They do not affirm themself and so become renowned. They do not brag, and so they accomplish. They are not self-satisfied, and so they are the head. They never dispute, and so across the whole world no one can dispute with them. They dare to not even eat a peach and thereby bring the overwhelming question.

No wonder "crookedly complete" was the motto of the ancients!

11

One does not stand firm on tiptoes. One does not trek by doing lunges.

They who show off are not famous. They who affirm themself are not renowned. They who brag do not accomplish. They who are self-satisfied are not the head.

This behavior is like a tumor, a useless addition to the movement that kills the movement. One who is following the course does not abide with it.

12

The Activist has no Cartesian mind, twinkling, independent, and pristine in its solitude. The Activist takes the mugged mind of the mass—the actual mass, not the false mass of theory.

By losing themselves in the mass, the Activist holds faith with the mass.

If they could only bind society in a cloud of unknowing, until the ears filled up and the eyes flamed out, there would be no goal unmet.

13

The professional organizers read this book, and they think that the course I am describing is a giant nothing. They are correct: it is a nothing because it is giant. Things that are at their scale exist for them: a water bottle, a tent, a barricade, an enemy. For most of human history, no one suspected the existence of the universe, because it is beyond our scale.

I have three secret weapons in my advocacy. The first is sympathy for those who oppose me. The second is simplicity of my life and my asks. The third is never, ever seeking to lead.

Sympathy gives me the courage to engage in persuasion rather than shouting from behind my physical or emotional barricades. Simplicity gives me the capital to extend the scope and the reach of my movement. Never seeking to lead gives me the power to lead administrators and police wherever I want them to go.

If I were to trade in sympathy for a willingness to shake things up, I would end up in the emergency room, angrily self-satisfied, and I would be no closer to my goal. If I were to trade in simplicity for good funding and complex planning, I would be thought of as the tool of hostile foreign forces, and I would be no closer to my goal. If I were to trade in my unwillingness to lead for a place of primacy, then everyone would know that my own interest is in myself, and I would be no closer to my goal.

Of these three, the chief is sympathy. Attack in sympathy, and you will capture your enemies and make them your recruits. Defend in sympathy, and no blow will ever land on your army.

14

The greatest warrior does not go to war. The greatest soldier does not indulge in anger. The greatest conqueror does not ever join battle with the enemy. The greatest user of human capital humbles themself before their colleagues.

This is called "the power of nonaggression." This is called "the force of using people correctly." This is called "accommodating oneself to the utter extremities of the ancient universe."

15

There is a saying about how to lead an army: "Don't be a subject, be an object." Feint forward and then fall back to wait. This is called progress without progression, preparing without preparations, grabbing the enemy without an enemy, and seizing the military without a military.

There is no greater danger than in underestimating your enemy. Underestimating your enemy will cost you your greatest treasure. When joining battle, the victor will be the one who begins already prone on the ground, weeping for fallen comrades.

16

Knowing one's ignorance is supreme; being ignorant of one's knowledge is a disease. Only in calling a disease a disease can one be free of the disease. The Activist does not have this disease, because they know to call the disease diseased.

17

Someone who is brave enough to be bold will rush into the vanguard and get cut down. Someone who is brave enough to be cowardly will hang back toward the rear and will live a long, happy life. This is just the course of how things go, and one can see what the universe loves and what it hates. Who can second-guess the way things are?

This is why the Activist recognizes some things as hard. Adhering to the universal course, they know that it is easy to win when one does not contend, it is easy to answer when one does not speak well, it is easy to set a trap when the net hangs loose.

The weaving of the nets set by the universe is the loosest and widest, but nothing can ever slip through it.

18

No substance on earth is as weak as water, which is why the authorities blast it from water cannons. Even those who would control for the purpose of harm know the force of water. The weak always overcomes the strong, and the yielding overcomes the steadfast.

This is easy to see and hard to practice, because your emotional firmware is organized differently. An outrage must be met with outrage, and violence calls forth violence.

Therefore, the Activist says: The one who collects filth is the one capable of being the planter of the garden. The one who collects humiliation is the one who deserves to be called president of the world.

The real text is always written on the back of the page.

Resting

1

LOAF AND INVITE YOUR SOUL TO THE GRASS AT A QUIET BEND IN the course. Wherever you drew the atoms of your blood, whether you are foreign to the place where you stand, you are native to that bend, as was your every ancestor. Because that is no land, it has always been your own and never only your own. But like as not, you will have it to yourself for as long as you want to stay.

That is the place to sit and to forget. Take in your mind, like a waistband you have shrunken from: bring it back down to your gut. Reduce the ghosts of existence to the space of perception; reduce the wraiths of your psyche to the space of perception. Do not worry that this sitting by the bend is a delay or a detour from your goal; the course is the only way to your goal.

When you have learned to reduce yourself to your self, you are ready to begin.

2

It is difficult to say nonwords and to perform nonactions. Most protestors not only cannot do this, but they also cannot understand it, cannot imagine it, and cannot accept it. And so, they continue to flail, chained to appearances, tortured by emotion.

One can only start to say nonwords and to perform nonactions by keeping oneself rooted in the nonexistent. Keeping oneself rooted in the nonexistent is the way to see the nonexistence of the self and the nonexistence of others, the nonexistence of the end and the nonexistence of the means.

Only when one sees these nonexistences can one understand the thin rim of their real existence. From a settled mind it is easier, then, to say nonwords and to perform nonactions and to see them through to the end.

3

The mind is the suzerain of the body and the commandant of the spirits. When it is quiet, then it bears wisdom, but when it moves it grows confused. Do you understand the vanity of taking delight in the realms of fantasized justice and of believing that words can contain realities?

Disordering the relation of mind and perception comes from entrusting your mind and perception to the wrong places. Good comrades make you more harmonious, and good teachers make you more upright. How much more so if your body leaves behind the realms of life and death, and you settle your mind on the course—won't you take on the character of what is around you? Therefore, when you begin to learn the course, it is necessary to sit peacefully and gather in your mind. Leave behind the physical world to settle in Nothing; having settled in Nothing, you will not be attached to a thing and will enter of yourself into the void, where your mind may unite with the course.

4

Who can integrate body and mind, living in the hinge of the cerebellum? Who can breathe with the softness of the infant? Who can polish the dust of deeply felt plots from off their field of vision? Who can guide their movement without a hint of cognition? Who can bring the filthy spirit of the anus right up to the heavenly gates of the telos?

Only the Activist. They give birth and nourish. They give birth but do not own. They act without name. They lead without directing. This is what is called "murky sway."

5

In its original structure, the mind has its origin in the course; but it becomes stained and obscured by long contact with the emotions, wanders for long days, and is eventually cut off from the course. That cutting off is like snapping an intestine in two.

But if one cleans out the muck of the mind and opens the apertures of the origin, this is called "practicing the course." If one leaves off from wandering, unites with the course in the depths, and rests upon it, this is called "returning to the root." Holding onto that root, not separating from it, this is called "quietly settling." When one has quietly settled for a long time, diseases will dissipate, and life will be restored, and you will naturally attain understanding of the constant.

This knowledge will leave nothing unclear, and the constant has nothing that can be destroyed. Truly, this is the way to leave behind success and failure, like a wild goose abandoning autumn frontiers. For that reason, practice the course and pacify your mind, and value nonattachment. Only then will you start to separate means from ends.

6

Grasp the outline of the universal, and the world will follow; following, they will not be harmed, and peace will be magnified.

A catchy protest song might lure some bystanders wandering over, but on the course one sings a chanty of no tone, and that non-melody cannot be unheard.

Sit at the confluence, beyond the boundaries, where the mountains hang between "there" and "gone."

7

Thirty spokes gather at the hub, because the hub is empty.

The use of the backpack is its emptiness. The use of the encampment tent is its space. The use of the water bottle is its hollowness. The use of the hard drive is its blankness. The use of the doorway is its vacuity. The use of the bullhorn is the open air.

The Activist is also useful through his emptiness. Holding a void in one's mind is what allows one to carry the cause.

8

In saying that the Activist must keep their mind empty, I do not mean that they tie down their mind in residence at the great palace of Emptiness. If you are thinking of "Emptiness," then that becomes a thing, and you are no longer empty. Lodging your mind within a concept is a way to exhaust it, as it runs counter to the nature of mind—you'd make yourself sick that way.

Only when the mind is unattached to any object or any concept can it attain stillness, and this is the true way to settle it upon a square foundation. When the mind is as empty of Emptiness as it is of Plans, Preparations, Tactics, and Organization, then it has room for the course to run through it. One can safely follow that course back to the goal only when one has forgotten how to have a concept.

9

There was an ancient Activist who knew the perfect course: a miracle, an unknown Knower.

They can't be described, so I can only describe them like this: Reluctant like an elderly driver pulling into traffic, stuttering like a witness to genocide, embarrassed like an honoree, delicate as April ice. They were raw lumber. Empty and muddy as a wastewater delta in a dead marsh.

That is the Activist, and that is the perfect course: never taking the smallest step toward the goal, one has already arrived as the movement's Martyr.

10

You can know the world without opening your phone, understand the course without opening Windows. The farther you browse, even in analog, the less you will reach.

Therefore, the Activist knows without scrolling, touches without swiping, achieves without doing.

11

The course has never yet run through a digital space.

The online world is not evil, but it is mostly unhealthy. It is the opposite of emptiness: all stimulus, all attachment, all perception rendered in blue light, endless addiction to avatarized emotion. The simulacrum on the screen is always an edit, masquerading as unmediated experience. Comment threads descend inexorably into argument and anger because there is no chance to look into the face behind a stupid comment—the face would make a total claim upon us, for calmness and kindness.

Detachment, withdrawal, stopping the ears, and blinding the eyes—these are the ways to power down.

12

Follow the void to its end and hoard silence.

Everything and everyone around me explodes in a violent concatenation of gestures and shouts, with the decibels teeming like lemmings, and objects and people tripping over each other in a riot of some sort in which joy and injury cannot be separated and may never have been not one thing.

And I watch them.

Going back to your phenomenological roots is the kind of silence that is called "reliving." Reliving is a constancy, and knowing that constancy is smart. Before the hurly-burly's done, just wander off with your feet or with your mind, breathe from the center, at the margin. Perhaps the hurricane will re-form around you, its eye, and perhaps it won't. But in the constancy of your rediscovered life, you may act freely and achieve.

13

Understand gender but protect what is ungendered in you. Be the sewer of the world, and the world will flow down into you, and you will never be separated from power. Understand illumination but protect what is unilluminated in you. Be the empty mold of the world, and the world will be pressed into your shape, and you will never be lacking in power. Understand respect but protect what is disrespected in you. Be the rut of the world, and the world will roll along the course you have become, and your power will be sufficient.

Be the raw lumber. Because when lumber gets carved, it is carved into tools, and those tools are used by the Administrators of the Way Things Are.

14

Do not be a tool of the state. Do not be a tool of the protest leader. Do not be a tool of your tactics. Do not be a tool of yourself.

To avoid becoming a tool, you must slough off your social role and preserve what is human; then you must unzip your humanity and find what is prior to your being human. Root yourself in the bare ground of what is and learn to vegetate there, eating the light.

It is when you allow yourself to be cut down, sawed, shaped, pressure washed, treated, locked, and shipped that you become lumber, material for the carver. At that point it is too late not to be carved into a tool, and you will be made to serve whoever grabs you.

15

Knowing people is crafty, but knowing oneself is intelligent. Conquering others is forceful, but conquering oneself is strong. Perseverance is ambitious, but contentment is success. Not losing your shelter along the course is to survive: the longevity of death without disappearance.

Therefore, you lotus of countless petals: unfold yourself to yourself.

16

The cosmos started, framed by the parentage of time and space. In that blank space of relation, they knew each other, parents and child, with no affection and no rancor.

Return to those parents, as a cell of the cosmos; shut firmly all the gates of perception, and you will be at rest all the days of your life.

Emancipate yourself from them, in a rush to the violent engagements of locked words and bitter hands, and you will burn off like brandy from a cherry.

17

The framework of the dimensions does not age, because it does not enter into the solaces and rues of those busy within it.

That is the secret of Being: one lives forever by not living.

Therefore, the Activist absents themself from the cause: no passion and no frustration. They allow themself to be a blank universe in which the cause unfolds.

Being something other than a human, they can at last accomplish the goals of the human.

18

Go ahead, go ahead down into the little drain holes at the bottom of yourself. It is not so hard to flow there as you might think. Close your eyes and count to eight, and you will already be gone. You will leave behind the detritus of what you had thought you had hoped to be, but that will not be your concern. Someone might be along to clean, or not.

Having flown down and out from yourself, you will join with other little flows and move downward. Joining with them is a kind of justice, though not what you had thought it would be. Moving out under the stars and into the oceans of non-distraction, non-excitement, non-care, and nonbeing, you will find yourself ready to fly at nothing.

And all the forces that stood against you, mocking, will also come to nothing. The mountains and rivers will stay behind.

Nothing

1

THE MOTION OF THE COURSE IS: RETURNING. THE USE OF THE course is: weakness.

All beings in the cosmos are born from "is," but "is" is born from "isn't."

2

The Buddhists say: not something and not nothing. Not something and nothing. And not neither something nor nothing. That is a great way to describe it from the outside, from within the world of something where technical logic happens.

What it feels like to the Buddha-nature walking the course is: the ripple left by a lotus petal in the stream, after it has propagated past the waterfall.

3

The great course is broad, plenty of room on the left and the right. Everything in the universe is nourished by it, and it cannot refuse them. It gives them all the necessaries of Being without ruling.

It has no desires—does that make it "small"? It contains all—does that make it "great"?

Perhaps it is great—but only by never claiming greatness.

It cannot claim greatness because it is not a thing that "is." The course is not a god, or a spirit, or a presence, or even an absence. One does not have to believe in things to believe in it. That is why it can serve as the nourisher of things that are and why it can settle down into the fundament of time and space.

4

The course to follow goes nowhere and reaches everywhere: it lies askew to the street you meant to take and that would only have taken you to another street.

Plant nine fields of orchids and a hundred acres of sweet basil. Let no one see or smell them and harvest them only in your own time.

Deflate the balloon, un-ice the cake, return the gift, and this course where no one walks will host the party.

5

You could perfectly understand the nature of nothing without leaving the world, but you would not want to. That is the way of antisocial personality disorder: no attachments because no mirror neurons, lies and crimes, coldness and risk. It isn't the profile of those who set out to repair the world.

To repair the world, it is best to see through it first: look at its reverse side, not at its seductive front. This is only the healthy psychopathy of the phenomenological reduction, pitilessly cutting away the supposition of existence to see things as they truly are not. When you understand your perception as perception, in all its noncommittal flash, you are already well on your way.

6

Stared at and unseen: the Planed. Heard and unlistened: the Wispy. Grabbed and unfelt: the Micro.

These things cannot be perceived, but they can be known. They have their source in a kind of Being—call it a subject of Science. It is the most universal, and the most present of grounds: filaments of energy and matter laced through vacuum.

What we can see, hear, and touch is a sick joke with a silent punchline. Haze and ghosts are the full substance of our Being.

Hold fast to the emptiness of the equations, running in miraculous skein through history to the future. Follow it out of the maze.

7

The Activist and the Agitator walked into a bar. The Agitator said, "I'll take your entire stock of top-shelf liquor" and proceeded to take down the bottles and drink without waiting for the bartender to reply. The Activist looked at the bartender somewhat sheepishly, and said, "Nothing for me, thanks."

By the middle of the second bottle, the Agitator had passed out flat on the floor. The Activist rolled him onto his side for safety and finished his drinks.

8

The constant course never does anything, and so there is nothing it cannot do. It is because the Activist holds and keeps it that all of society can transform itself. If after transformation it would revert toward desire, they just pin it lovingly under the weight of the raw lumber. The lumber does nothing but settle desire and, again, society settles into peace.

Doing nothing is not the same as being nothing. But one has to embody the possibility of being nothing to be the lumbery something that knows how to do nothing.

9

Don't think that you can just point to nothing. A black hole seems to be the nothingest nothing there is, but it is the somethingest something. Wait one hundred trillion years, to when it has evaporated, and then it might only be nothing much.

Going around in your mind, looking for the biggest nothing you can see, is a misdirection. Fortunately, nothing has always been around, in, and through you: less like outer space and more like plain old space, with a z-axis. Not math itself, and not something math can describe, but you could describe it as being something like math could describe.

The best way to see nothing is slantwise while failing to find a something. It will light up like moss on a tree trunk in the late afternoon.

10

When the Activist hears of the course, they recognize that they have never not been using it. When the best worker hears of the course, they labor diligently to put it into practice. When the average worker hears of the course, they try it out a bit when it seems to fit. When the bad worker hears of the course, they do a spit take and start ragging on it. It wouldn't be the course if it didn't get that kind of treatment from each kind of person. This is why the ancient protest chant makers would shout the following:

Hey, ho, what's the course?
    It seems weak but it's got force!
Hey, ho, where's the course?
    Everywhere, it is the source!
Say its name!
    It has no name!
What does it want?
    It makes no claim!
1, 2, 3, 4
    Nameless at its primal core!
5, 6, 7, 8
    We will just nickname it "great"!

Of course, they did not shout these slogans using their voices or for humans to hear. That would have just been silly.

11

Weight is what roots lightness; stillness is the controller of movement.

Therefore, the Activist travels the course all day without separating light from heavy: though magnificent airy prospects of victory appear just beyond their grasp, they stay planted in the space and time where they are.

If they let themselves float after victory, they would disconnect from their source; if they rushed the movement forward, they would lose control.

This is why the Activist knows how to use the "Heavenly Ballast." The Heavenly Ballast is what they load into the hull, after they have unloaded all the things of false value, demanded on the market. Heavy, worthless, and useless, the Heavenly Ballast brings the ship of the Activist down into the water, to the low level where it can steer without capsizing. This is how they keep the course.

12

There is an object that congealed out of chaos prior to the framework of time and space. Oh, so quiet, oh, so hollow, it is established sole and never reforms, rotating on with no loss of momentum. It could be the parent of the universe.

There's no good name for it, so I call it "the course" and nickname it "vast." Being vast, it lumbers off, far off, and then comes back: a course. The course is vast, time is vast, space is vast, and the Activist is vast. There are four vasts, but the Activist sits in the middle of them.

Humanity takes its cues from space, space takes its cues from time, time takes its cues from the course, and the course is the self-thus.

13

The course produces unity. Unity produces numbers. Numbers are for all that is.

All that is, is a combination in various proportion of various levels of various subatomic particles. Not just multiplicities, but multiplicities of multiplicities.

The Activist is no less a multiplicity, but by returning through unity to the course, they also know their own solitude. They do not mind labeling themself with the kinds of words that start fights: moron, freak, loser, asshole. Donate to them, and you hurt them; steal from them, and you make them whole.

14

How does the Activist remain planted in nothing while leading the protest?

Having learned how to rest on the course is part of it—staying there, unmoving, for kalpa after kalpa, one trades some of one's substance for nonsubstance, so it's much easier to carry the nothing along in a backpack.

Having learned how to see that everything is in the course, and is the course, is also part of it—then one can take objects and people more seriously than they take themselves and support them more easily than they can support themselves. It is easy to carry nothing.

Having learned how not to learn is also a part of it. One can then withdraw from the ideological construction of the self and the other into fantasy players upon a spare stage. Decouple all beings from the scripts with which you would program them, and they will revert to what they have always been.

Mostly, though, it's like this:

A clean rectangle on a camel wall while the movers load.

A kindergarten cubby, in un-air-conditioned August, while cicadas sing.

A feathery soufflé baked for a photo shoot.

A lobster trap set by a misled child in the shoals of the North Platte, forgotten through winters.

15

The course is constant and anonymous. Though raw lumber is mere matter, no one on earth can force it to serve. Though raw lumber is large and cumbersome, it can dodge without budging. Nothing else is required.

If the Activist holds on to the course, everything will align, time and space will cohere, and all of society will arrange itself in equity, with no laws or leaders. Only when administration begins can labels appear, and when there are labels, then it is time to stop and pull back, and then one is free again from danger. Do not let yourself be labeled, because you will first be labeled "labeler."

But the anonymous course still sits below the world and receives it the way the Pacific receives the thinnest Andean rivulet.

16

The unity of time is in motion. The unity of space is in stillness. The unity of life is in biochemistry. The unity of beings is in cognition. The unity of protestors is in the goal. The unity of protest leaders is in patience.

Without these unities that make them what they are, time would crumple to a freeze-frame, space would tear like a leaky bag, life would unwind itself into fuel, beings would lose themselves in perception, protestors would be well-hydrated 'Ndrangheta, protest leaders would burn.

This is why you must hold on to the source, even though the source is not a thing. It is low, it may have no other substance than the substantiality of position, but it is your foundation.

17

The course births it, power raises it, matter forms it, momentum completes it. This is why it loves the origin and admires the end: not because it is "nature," but because it is the nature of things.

There is something that brings it along from stage to stage, passing into maturity without aging or age. Like a parent, it does not expect thanks.

18

The course of time and space is to draw things toward evenness, like a bow being pulled taut: the top is lowered and the bottom raised while the thin middle grows spacious and round.

Entropy in the nature of things will cause organization to disappear. Gravity constantly pulls the whole of the planet toward a sphere. Erosion blasts grains off the mountaintops and feeds them to the trenches of the ocean.

Everywhere, nature is socialist, taking from where there is too much and delivering to where there is a lack. It is only humans (including Socialist humans) who take from those who lack and deliver to those who already have too much.

The Activist is socialist, whether or not they are Socialist. They smooth out the corners and fill in the gaps. They leave nothing that can be caught upon and snagged. This is how they accomplish the goal while absenting themself from the task.

Aiming

1

THE STEADY: EASY TO HOLD.

The unrevealed: easy to plot.

The crispy: easy to snap.

The wispy: easy to blow away.

Create a thing while it is still nothing and control a thing while it is still unmessy. The worst genocide develops out of a mild slur used in the market, and the most destructive war grows out of an argument over a suburban property line.

On the other hand, a protest march of a thousand miles begins underfoot, where one stands. The Activist can never fail because they never act, and if they do act, they only need to raise a finger and give the lightest push on a domino.

2

The time to end slavery was before the first slave ship wanted to dock; that would have cost a few arguments and a few hundred dollars. Instead, the United States waited until 1865, at the cost of billions of dollars, hundreds of thousands of lives lost in war, and millions of lives lost in slavery.

The time to end the Holocaust was after the Beer Hall Putsch; all that would have been required would have been not to let Hitler out of prison for "good behavior." But Germany waited and sacrificed its existence to exterminate half the Jews.

The time to end the Vietnam War was in 1961, when Kennedy first approved military involvement in Vietnam. When Saigon fell in 1975, 58,220 U.S. soldiers and three million Vietnamese had died to no discernible purpose at all.

Your protests will not end anything that has already swollen into a war. Try as hard as you can, and you will still be completely ineffective. Your protests can end something before an entire nation or an entire people has invested its wealth and its sense of self. The smaller the investment is now, the easier the divestment will be. Do not scorn to tackle a problem that does not yet have the romance of Great World-Historical Injustice. Fix the small things now, and you will save millions of future lives.

3

Speaking rarely is what makes one self-thus.

Strong gusts of wind can blow as much as they like, and then they have to stop. A downpour can make a flash flood, but the flood will drain away. These violences come with all the force of the framework of nature, but even nature has no permanent force. Why would a human?

This is why the Activist follows the course. In following the course, they become the course. In accepting power, they become power. In accepting loss, they become loss. When power or loss are not speakable for lack of words, one is equally content to get either and to become either.

Because that is not the point. The point is holding faith with the goal. Where there are no words, there can be no breach of faith.

4

When one does not hold faith with the goal, one holds faith with the oppressors.

If you wish to lift a siege from the outside, go to the site of the siege and harry the besieging army with archers and cavalry raids.

Even though your force may be small, you may be nimble. Burn their grain supplies and their trebuchets. Drop carcasses into their wells and drive plague victims to sleep in their tents. Do not stay at home and burn your own wheat fields on the theory that this will raise the price of wheat on world commodity markets and make it 0.1 percent more expensive for the besieging army to provision itself. You would achieve a great victory in complete safety over your own grain fields and then starve in your pride while your ally is sacked.

Ask yourself in the quiet places: what is the real goal, the ultimate goal? Seek the most direct course toward that goal; do not target an action by asking what is in reach. That is what the oppressors prefer: for you to make chaos in your home and stay out of their way.

5

Imagine ten comrades traveling down a road and coming to a fork. Three will take the left fork, toward living death; three will take the right fork, toward deadly life, and three will return on the road they came from, the Road of Nothing Much.

The Activist sits down at the crossroads and makes their home. The devil does not come to offer them any choice because the possibility of a choice was illusory: there was no choice, there was only a road. Being still on the road, knowing that no choice was made, the Activist can travel the course.

6

Weave the course into your tissues, and it will not be torn free; tuck it under the integument, tie it off on the epiphyses, and it will be stuck and strong.

Bring this in your person, and your power will be real. Bring it in your cell, and your power will be plentiful. Bring it in your movement, and your power will be long-lasting: four hundred years will pass by in a dream. Bring it in your society, and your power will be a harvest. Bring it in the world, and there will be no power, because no one will be without power.

The course has this power because it only travels in the right direction, in the right way. Those without it hack their own trails through the bush and exhaust themselves in order never to arrive.

7

When aiming the movement, the Activist retreats into solitude, and loneliness, and meditation in a bee-loud glade, and purges themself for at least a short eon. This is not a purge of the body; it is a fast of the mind, and it must be observed strictly. Too many phantoms of form hide the hungry ghosts; these must be warded off through deconstruction and ice. When the Activist has once again shed every concept, they will see clearly the true goal with true vision.

One of the ghosts to avoid is Sides. Sides are tool factories, taking in humans at industrial scale and outputting useful objects. They prevent protestors from seeing the true goal and direct them to the false goal called "Beating the Other Side."

One of the ghosts to avoid is Orthodoxy, the sneaky shade. Those who are most certain they have banished Orthodoxy are those on whose backs he most likes to dig his shadow claws. Orthodoxy steers you away from the goal by complaining about the road, but no wrong road parallels the course. The Activist beats Orthodoxy not by fighting Orthodoxy but by forgetting about him: the shade vanishes.

One of the ghosts to avoid is The People. Fight for what the people want, not what The People want. The People do not exist. If you persist in your idolatry of The People, you will end up throwing the people to them, as babies into the mouth of Āṭavaka.

But the most fearsome of the ghosts, the big boss, is Self. If you go into a protest carrying the idol of the Self around your neck, you will not be able to do what is necessary to reach the goal;

instead, you will do what is necessary to exalt yourself. This is not about self-sacrifice: those who self-immolate are the most deluded of all, sacrificing both the goal and the self to the Self.

Therefore, the Activist does not even remember their own existence and brews the completed goal into a nice herbal tea.

8

The Agitator sets up a book tent in the middle of the protest, but the Activist forgets how to read.

In the book tent, the Agitator has placed many volumes that will be useful in carving his comrades into tools: *The History of Our Great Cause*, *101 Reasons Why We Are Right*, *The Great Evil Done Evilly by Our Evil Enemy*, *A Critical Reader of Usbeingthegoodguys Theory*, and *Handy Handweapons for the Peaceful Protestor*. The comrades spend their downtime reading these and recharging their wrath so that they may become maximally clever and tenacious in doing battle against what they hope to achieve. In contrast, the Activist sits apart and reads nothing. They lie on the sweet, heartless grass and stay for a month after the protest has been beaten down and cleared; when they get up and stretch, the goal is attained.

Study is a progress, but activism is a regress: day by day, backward step behind step, until one backs up sightless into the goal.

9

When the people do not fear the might of the state, the might of the state will arrive. Do not put pressure on leaders in their homes; do not clamp down upon their means of living. Do not dox the trolls, and do not deplatform them—but also do not reply, and do not repost. Let their words thud dimly in space, muffled like a shout into a blizzard.

This is why the Activist knows themself without revealing themself, loves themself without valuing themself.

They take what's needed and shit out the rest.

10

When protestors are not afraid of arrest, why threaten them with arrest? If they were afraid of arrest, and the police could disperse them by threatening them with arrest, there would be no need to threaten.

On the other hand, when police are not afraid of making arrests, why prod them into making arrests? If they were afraid of making arrests, and you could make them back off by telling them how many phone cameras are pointed at them, they would never have showed up at the protests in the first place.

Viral videos do not show what you think they show. You and those who already agree with you can only see your own heroism. Those who have not yet made up their minds can only see that you are making it hard for them to go about their lives.

Trust that the course is the master carpenter. If you shove aside the master carpenter, and take over the work, you will just end up chopping off a finger.

11

No peace treaty will leave either side content; there will be lingering resentments and unfulfilled hopes. Similarly, no settlement achieved through protest will come close to the goal. Reaching one quarter of the goal is already an unheard-of achievement. But if you teach them to expect four quarters, this will leave the protestors dispirited and demoralized.

The Activist takes what they can get and does not linger on the three-quarters ungot. They do not let the hotheads sabotage the quarter with demands for the three-quarters. After the next round, the state will only be left with nine-sixteenths, then twenty-seven sixty-fourths. Learn to progress asymptotically. Always let the powerful win each round, and you will get all you want.

The bare framework of time and space does not have a sense of justice and does not play favorites. It gives to those who follow the course.

12

Maximal demands can be felt as righteousness and purpose or thought of as a smart opening bid; but deep in the recesses of the gonads they are known as the way to prevent the death of desire.

If your goal is the true goal, then you will work toward the goal. If your goal is to have a goal, then you will sabotage your goal. The politicians understand this: "Do you want the win or the issue?" If they refuse to solve the problem, they can continue to whip their side to anger that the problem is unsolved. The Activist wants the win, but the Agitator wants the issue—so that he can continue to win the vote of his id.

13

If you could rule the world and tried to implement change from above, you would fail. The world is a tool for gods; people who wield it get unexpected results. Even if you tried to grab just a little corner of the world, it would bobble out of your hands.

The world is a mess in which leaders are created by followers, those in ease are created by those who labor, the strong are created by the weak, and murderers are created by those they murder.

The Activist has no desire to be a creation of their own crime; that is why they avoid persistence, perfectionism, and bold stands.

14

Why are you traumatizing yourself and others on behalf of a goal that is no goal? The people of that faraway place will not be saved by your fighting online over definitions. No university divestment would block the howitzer shells. Disinviting a keynote speaker with the wrong name cannot unsow the salt from the fields.

Do you think you are doing your small part? You are doing less than nothing; your aim discredits your cause.

Do you think you are keeping pure? There is no purity in this world: you are made of the same shit that makes up all those who suffer and their oppressors. It will still be in your name; it is always in your name.

Do you do something because you can't do nothing? But you are wrong: you can do nothing, and sometimes you must—if you want to help, rather than to pose and harm.

15

In life, the human body is soft and flexible; only when it is dead does it wither. In life, grasses, leaves, and branches are elastic and supple; only when they are dead do they grow hard and brittle. Therefore, firmness and inflexibility are the way of death, but pliancy and yielding are the way of life.

A firm demand will not be met, and a hard thrust will only injure you. Instead, be as soft and yielding as water, and you will carry everything before you like a tsunami.

16

How does demanding too much of what is right prevent what is right? Because you anger the person of whom you demand it. If you would not meet a demand, why do you think that your demands will be met? You do not need the course to understand this; remedial kindergarten would suffice.

I hear you say: It is not my job to be polite; it is their job to do what needs doing. This is what is called "the drunk driver blaming the tree." In fact, no one has a job, and no one has a role. These are illusions with no substance. Rid yourself of illusion, cast a cold eye on life and death, and then you can begin to aim with true vision.

To aim true, you must understand those of whom you seek redress. Listen to what they say rather than what is said about them. Read what they write rather than what is written about them. Talk to them, as a human to a human, and there is a chance you might persuade them; if you cannot persuade them, you will still better understand their strengths and their weaknesses, which actions might help your cause and which would certainly hurt.

This is how the course succeeds in weakness.

17

The great course is nothing to be feared. It is a great highway, paved and smooth, eight lanes for a single pedestrian. It is strange that most of the protestors prefer the mazes of tiny little trails curving in hooks through the scrubland.

On those trails: there are many bottles of water and few new wells; there are many pizzas and few sacks of flour; there are many flags and few children's shoes; there are many placards and few constitutions.

This is the great theft: stealing from those whom one thinks one helps.

18

It is said that long ago the Queen Mother of the West lived in a palace in the Kunlun Mountains. There she had an orchard in which grew a peach tree. The peach tree bore fruit once every three thousand years, but if one could eat one of those peaches, one could gain immortality. Over the years, many intrepid Daoists, sorrowful at the ending of spring, would see the Queen Mother's messenger crows and take them as invitations to the banquet tables of Master Red Pine. Full of renewed hope, they each set out to those fearsome and distant mountains to obtain a peach, and all their bones lie gently in the sands of the Tarim Basin. The newer ghosts don't complain, nor do the older ones cry.

Don't quest.

Strategizing

1

THE ACTIVIST IS THE STRATEGIST, BUT THE AGITATOR IS THE tactician. The Agitator works hard to perfectly organize the protest, runs pre-protest meetings, assigns roles, gets media training, calls for food and water teams, writes do and don't lists, schedules speakers, checks the sound system, calls the assignment desk, forms an inner core of advisers, gets social media accounts set up and coordinated for maximum blast, and draws up an ideological line. All those tasks are executed properly, the team moves in unison, the message is picked up everywhere, and the government says no.

The only thing the Activist does is to realize clearly what change they want to see in the world. They only saunter toward that change but take no diversions. Going straight at the goal, all they need to do is whisper a request in the ear of a Tsing-ling pika, and even that whisper brings success.

2

The bling of good visuals brings blindness. The hard bass of the smart chant delivers deafness. The delicious martyrdom of the fast is fattening.

The electric energy of the hunt drives one mad: if the hunt is a Bacchic delirium, one prolongs the hunt and forgets the quarry.

Is the goal your goal? Or do you enjoy the party and the specter of purpose?

The Activist seeks the goal and trashes the tools. Freed from the tools, it is easy to attain the goal.

3

To have the perfect strategy, you must begin with perfect vision. To have the perfect vision, you must clear your mind of ideology and inspiration. Ideology and inspiration tell you that you cannot see clearly without them; they lie. These things only create heuristic shortcuts that cause you to ignore evidence.

Not all problems can be solved. No protest movement or violent uprising could have brought down the Third Reich from the inside. Sometimes evils can be stopped, sometimes they can only be slowed, and sometimes they can only be hastened. Being able to see and understand this clearly is the only way to begin.

Look for the field in which action can help and take only the action that will help. Look for the field in which nonaction can help and practice only the nonaction that will help.

4

Knowing theories is the highest knowledge, knowing methods is lower, knowing facts is lower, knowing the world is lower, knowing people is lower, knowing oneself is lower, knowing nothing is lower, not knowing how to know is the lowest.

Like water, flow down from the highest to the lowest. The lowest point is the greatest, the ocean of knowledge. In the profoundest depths so far from cleverness, one will know everything one needs for success.

5

Unlinking arms will keep the horses in their stables; dispersing for the bullhorn will sheath the club; melting away will undo the hopes of the fascists.

Therefore, in ruling over the government that attacks them, the Activist will give him nothing to hit, nothing to arrest, nothing to see. Keep the TV bored and make no one scared: then the message is everywhere; it is normal.

This is how one undoes the lie, through compliance.

6

Do not fill the wineglass to the very lip: it will spill, it will stain; you will drink nothing and enjoy less than nothing. Do not sharpen the pencil to a perfect mathematical point: you will waste its body in the quest for what cannot be and would self-destruct if it could be.

There is such a thing as perfect protest momentum: it dissipates. Your only choice is in how it will dissipate: partial victory or reactionary regression. Activists stop when they have gone one-quarter of the way to the goal. Set a marker where no one is threatened and then sleep: the mountain grows one inch per year.

7

Those who hold militant tactics a lovely thing—they are disastrous and detestable tools.

The Activist leans to the left when the Agitator leans to the right. They do not use the same methods.

If the Activist is ever forced into using the tactics of the Agitator, he does so in semiconscious blandness, never finding anything bracing or beautiful about them. Delight in conflict can only take one farther from the goal. A bear that develops a taste for human blood must be put down by the ranger; a comrade who develops a taste for conflict must be put out of the circle by the Activist. Lean to the left, never to the right.

If you ever seem to have won through conflict, cry deeply and cry quickly, because you must hide from what is coming.

8

If you ask, "Do these means justify this end?" then you have already lost.

A movement is not an ethics seminar. To ask ethical questions is to apply the wrong category, because you have never understood what you are doing. To say this is not to say that the end always justifies the means; it is to say that the word "justify" is a delusion, a self-imposed nothingness.

It would be somewhat better to ask, "Do these means promote this end?" That, at least, springs from an understanding of what you are doing: seeking a goal. If you have chosen a correct end, of ultimate value, then no form of violence—or even a rude word—will ever promote the end. Through total amorality, you would become what the moralists call a "saint."

But it would be better still not to know even what "means" means. Thinking about means is not a means that promotes the end. Be spontaneously simple, withdrawn, soft, weak, and natural, and you will neither understand nor need any means. You will just be what you are, never distracted by tactics, and will tumble into the end that you need.

9

To shrink injustice, stretch it to vast and perfect thinness. To weaken evil, pump it full of steroids. To pop a system, incite it to swell with pride. To seize accounts, gain access through donations.

This is smart subtlety: to conquer through yielding. Always be the attacked, not the attacker. Always be the humiliated, not the humiliator. Always be the punching bag, absorbing blows with a thud, uncomplaining, swinging slightly under received momentum.

Do not even appear to have a mind or a purpose. Do have a mind and a purpose, but do not show it to anyone, except occasionally to yourself. The Activist is a flounder, skimming the ocean floor, never rising to where they can be fathomed.

10

They who wish to aid society do not try to force its behavior through militancy. If you have a goal, do not think of your movement as an army. An army is a thing that explodes three babies for every enemy combatant. An army decamps from fields of toxic smoke and meat sauce.

Therefore, do not execute your protest operations with military precision or tight organization. Be only as organized as the tides, ebbing up in gentle liquid rhythms, then going slack and wandering away. It is enough to leave a line, for a few hours, at the high-tide mark.

11

Which is most important, your reputation or your physical existence? Which is most valuable, your financial assets or your emotional existence? Which is a bigger benefit, profit or loss?

When you start to accumulate, you begin to incur costs: security, insurance, storage fees, or hedging investments; and still there is the cost of risk, which cannot be eliminated.

When a movement grows, it also incurs costs: person hours, organizational structures, reactionary enemies, creeping bureaucracy; and still there is the cost of lost control, which cannot be eliminated. Do not judge your strength by the size and reach of your organization; judge your strength by your ability to reach your goal. A single TikTok recorded in your bedroom might have all the reach you need, and a single meeting with the right decision-maker might have all the persuasion you need.

This is why the Activist knows when to stop, whether in acquiring capital or comrades. If you choose the right spot, it can be enough to lie down on the bare ground, naked, with a friend.

12

When the attainment is imperfect, it won't be reversed. When there is leakage from the goal, it stays full.

Real toughness is flabby, real armor is shabby, real rhetoric is babbly. If you look to improve your tools and methods, your mind will be on your tools and methods. If you do not care for your tools and methods, you will be liberated from distractions. Then you will be able to attune yourself to your goal, and the optimal strategy for reaching the goal will become clear.

Heat does not reach the depths of a cave: being still and clear as a vile pool is how one riles society right.

13

A great movement is like the siltlands below New Orleans, the place where all the continental waters of justice flow. It can receive them because it sits low, in the gathering place by the Gulf, the framework of time and space.

The large movement, taking the lower place, absorbs the smaller movement; the smaller movement, in moving downward, gains the clout of the larger movement. The one wants to take on, and the other wants to be taken on.

"Solidarity" is too weak a word for it; "intersectionality" is dippy: call it the Universal Delta.

14

In a small protest with few people, leave at home all the tools needed for a protest and make sure that everyone fears arrest too much to act rashly. Even if someone brings placards, do not use them; and if someone starts taking video, ask them not to upload or share it.

Make all the protestors pristine and preliterate, as if they barely know how to draw or speak. Do not organize them and do not even have a planned action for the protest.

And if you happen to hear of another protest one subway stop away, do not go over to join them, and do not coordinate. Be like Neolithic villages that barely traded, though close enough to hear each other's roosters crow.

15

Kill your machine mind.

The machine mind is the renegade android of your frontal cortex, rewiring fears of the hindbrain into calculations and plots. Many plans to keep you awake, many visualizations of move after countermove. This is the one who makes you stare into the distance, thinking of what you should have said. This is the one who eats barbs.

When you kill your machine mind, you free yourself to leave the game of traps that you've set yourself. Then you can start to look out at the vistas, where your real goal lies.

16

Being trained in nonviolence as a tactic is good, but it is barely the first step upon the course. Nonviolence cannot itself be used as a form of violence or it will slide back into violence. Nonviolence is not employed to cleverly trick the cameras into thinking that you do not wish to bash in the heads of the fascists. Nonviolence is not a trick, it is not a scheme, it is not a tactic. You cannot call for bloody violence with your lungs, have your hands open and weapon free, and expect that violence will not have been felt by anyone who has heard you.

The nonviolence of the Activist is nonviolent to the innermost core. The only tactical nonviolence they use is upon their own emotional structure that wants to yield to the desire to inflict pain. When that has been conquered, there will be no more enemies who need conquering. They will sit down with you and talk with you, and you will sway them to your side.

17

Violence is not violence. Conflict is violence. If you wish to be nonviolent, you must be non-conflictual.

Watch a Muay Thai fight. Combatants use far more devastating violence, unarmed, than any protestor could with bats or Molotov cocktails. They beat each other bloody, break bones, tear cartilage, harm brains. And yet the combatants enter the ring with respect and leave it with affection, hugging and leaning upon each other. The winner is not arrogant, and the loser is not humiliated. This is because their violence is not conflict, it is sport.

Think now of your own worst family conflict where no one raised anything but a voice. Your bones were not broken, and your skin was not torn. Yet the scars of that violence are with you until today—in the things that you cannot do, the places you cannot go, the people you cannot meet, the words you cannot hear. If you have healed, you still understand the toll that that nonviolent violence took; if you have not healed, then you may still not understand because you cannot start to think about it without feeling the adrenaline death. How can nonviolence have been so violent? Because hate was where there should have been love, threat where there should have been safety.

Therefore, do not think that you have practiced nonviolence when you touch no one but scream at them to die. To practice nonviolence, practice non-conflict. Tell your enemies that you love them and wish them long life. Then they will listen to you, and you will win.

18

In the world of political action, there can be no sole forces. Anything new will create its opposite, Eve called forth from Adam's side. Protest calls forth counterprotest. Occupation calls forth cops. Leftists call forth rightists. Justice calls forth injustice. Genocide calls forth counter-genocide. Walk this route, and there is only the Manichean struggle all the way down the whirlpool.

There is no way to escape this cycle by pushing harder. More forceful action calls forth the more forceful response. The binary will still be binary. The two sides of the equation must always remain in balance.

One escapes by escaping: stop the action, and you cut off the counteraction. Leave off, go home, and your enemies will wander off like cottonwood fluff in a June zephyr.

Leading

1

A HUMAN IN THIS WORLD IS LIKE A TICKET STUB, AND SO THE Activist treats his comrade like a ticket stub: already torn, no need to tear, good for a memento.

Where is the venue that the memento recalls? Here, around us, the empty Odeon of the lapsed Paleozoic. We were never whole, and none of us were ever masters.

No wonder that the bare architecture of space and time, always and everywhere giving, shows through in the face of the comrade. This is why the Activist does not organize and is not organized: we can never have been each other's tickets into the full life. There is nowhere to enter except where we are now.

2

The best leader of the movement is one whom no one realizes is the leader. After that comes the one whom they follow from respect. After that comes the one who makes them uncomfortable. After that comes the one who causes splintering.

Mutual trust can only be lost when one starts speaking, so the best leader hardly speaks.

One day, the goal is attained, and then they all say, "But we didn't do anything at all!"

3

A good king is a desiccated thing, gesturing a bit from his chair. A quarterback leads his team by retreating: moving backward, behind the line of scrimmage, to where he can see the field, direct, and assess. A general leads a battle by descending into a bunker, receiving data from many fronts, then deciding where the next round of deployments would be most effective. A queen ant leads her colony from the deepest recesses of the nest, receiving tribute, producing eggs, and emitting her directives through chemical secretions without ever moving from her throne.

Alpha dogs are dogs.

4

Kick out the courageous from the movement, and everyone left will have real courage. Drive the self-sacrificing away from your protest, and there will be no need for sacrifice. Turn your backs on any hopeful fucker, and the goal will already have been reached. Remember, hope is a road that returns to nature simply by not walking on it.

Anything that stinks of virtue must be flushed if you want any progress. Don't move anyone to tears; don't stir a flicker of righteous emotion. Those are distractions, seducing you away from the goal and to the process.

Be naked and cold as one abandoned before dawn, the raw lumber. Anything else is a pose and a betrayal.

5

To move swiftly, leave no ruts. To speak well, leave no hooks for argument. To be good at math, don't count on your fingers. To be good at locking a door, leave it open. To be good at tying a knot, throw away the rope.

This is why the Activist is good at saving people—they just don't discard people. It is why they are good at saving things—they just don't discard things. This is called "hiding your lamp under a bushel."

Someone who is good with people seems to be a leader to someone who is bad with people, but someone who is bad with people seems to be an object to be used to someone who is good with people. This is not the course of the Activist, who neither leads nor uses, is neither led nor used.

6

Manage the movement by openness, be clever in dodging conflict on the way to the goal, and win over society by not forcing society. The more shibboleths you enforce, the more you lock yourself off from those you need to persuade. The more you talk to each other, the more you will talk over your friends on the outside. The more you hide behind barricades, the more you limit your vision. The more you secure your tactics, the more you will let slip your strategy.

Therefore, the Activist says: I take no action, and society is transformed of itself. I prefer silence, and society hears the message of itself. I do not force society, and society forces itself. I am free from desire, and society becomes the same raw lumber I am.

7

When protest leadership is confused, the protest is pure. When protest leadership is alert, aware, on top of contingency planning, and tactically crafty, the protest is fraudulent.

The red-headed weaver perches upon the great baobab, but the elephant perches upon the thinnest of savannah grasses.

Chase your tendencies to the limit: you will see that the straight and unyielding warps like wet wood, the beautiful and beneficent ages into the demonic. The movements have been addled for many years now.

This is why the Activist is square like a circle, is bent with no corners, punches through to the end without a fist, and lights everything dimly.

8

In leading the actions of the movement, there is nothing like being stingy with force. This is called, "yielding early and often." When one yields early and often, one heaps up power. Heaping up power, nothing is left unsubdued. With nothing unsubdued, there is no definable endpoint. Without a definable endpoint, one can take the society, and then the source of the society, where the roots are and where the life comes from.

9

The leadership of the movement was contested, and it was decided that the Activist and the Agitator should run a race to determine who should lead. When the starter's pistol was fired, the Agitator dashed forward into a fast run, but the Activist moved cautiously, step-by-step, as if pacing through a set of tai chi forms. Leg swept past leg, twisting gracefully, and the Activist barely made any progress.

As the Agitator disappeared over the horizon, he looked back and saw that the Activist had barely progressed from the starting line. Therefore, he decided that he could take a long break and lay down under a shady oak to rest, outside of the heat of the day. He napped for an hour and then, feeling quite refreshed, resumed the race and passed the finish line first. He broke through the tape with his arms upraised, but no one was there to celebrate his leadership.

Back at the starting line, the Activist had moved forward about ten meters by the end of their tai chi routine. Though not at all fatigued from this exertion, the Activist had also lain down to nap. The rest of the protest movement, who had gathered at the starting line, were mesmerized by the Activist's graceful and weird movements so that by the time the Activist stretched out upon the ground, they saw that as an excellent idea, and they all lay down to sleep as well.

10

The weakest leader of the movement is the one who has consolidated all power and respect, makes all decisions, issues a command and sees it done, goes on television to represent his army, and is eventually elected to the legislature.

A less-weak leader chooses top lieutenants of strong commitment and ability, leads them in a council for decision-making, delegates authority to them, and makes sure that they lead their various divisions in precise steps, coordinating the effective execution of tasks.

A moderately weak leader engages the entire movement in building consensus, facilitates democratic decisions, and ensures only that the result is clear policies and directions that can then be enforced and implemented without favoritism.

A moderately strong leader works through decentralized online spaces that have no decisions or policies, only trends and spontaneous collaborations. They spread the word and go with the flow.

A stronger leader does not collaborate with anyone, online or off. Stronger leaders walk hesitatingly through a crowd with an air that attracts attention; though they don't say a word, everyone begins to follow them without understanding why.

The strongest leader of the movement has never known that there was a movement, nor have they met another human before. They sit alone in their apartment and look out at the street, inferring by the passage of cars that society exists. When they twitch an index finger once, history rewrites itself.

11

The course is the gyre of all things, the storehouse for those who do good to humans, but also the redeemer of those who do bad.

Rhetoric decorates, respect elevates, but where is the use in abandoning the bad?

When the Activist appoints their lieutenants, it is senseless to choose those who bring their technical skills as offerings: they choose instead the ones before their eyes, the ones who bring the course.

In ancient times, this was the reason why the course was valued: to attain the goal without suffering one's own faults.

12

The ancient ones who were good at following the course in their protests did not want to educate their comrades. Instead, they kept them ignorant.

A movement becomes unruly when everyone has their own idea. So, if you ask everyone to read, and to brainstorm, or even if you let them see you making crafty plans, the movement will fall apart.

If you organize the movement by making sure that no one has any ideas, then the movement will cohere in peace. This is called the Obscure Power.

13

All the fertile lands lay between the river and the sea, but it is the river and the sea that are their masters, not whoever rules them. The river and the sea exercise their mastery from below: they receive all that drains off, as tribute. They are the final home.

Therefore, whoever wants to rule between the river and the sea must likewise be the lowest. Whoever wants to lead the movement must walk in the rear.

The Activist can remain atop the movement because no one feels their weight. They can remain in front of the movement because no one takes offense. The movement is always content with them, and no one in the whole society can find a problem with them.

14

The reason protestors get exhausted is because their leaders ask too much of them. The reason protestors get crabby and argumentative is because their leaders set out too many tactical rules.

A bad leader likes to have their encampment exhausted and crabby, because it makes it easier to direct their wrath against the enemy, to defend the barricades against the counterprotesters.

A good leader likes to achieve the goal. The goal is not a fight.

15

Organizing a large movement is like sautéing a fish fillet: tend to it too much, and it will disintegrate.

If the course runs through your movement, then the Undead of the Id will not grow unquiet, they will not haunt your tents or grow hungry for brains.

Let those monsters sleep fitfully, but sleep: draw from their animal spirits without giving them votes. Then they will not harm your comrades nor society.

The Activist will do no harm.

16

An old poem says, "Geese are in flight, their feathers rustling; people are far off, sent to labor in the wilds."

The people are corvée laborers, at work upon fortifications predating the Great Wall; they owe the sovereign their labor and serve in bitterness. The geese are geese, self-sent and self-directed to the south, seeking warmth by instinct and needing no other nature than their own.

Do you want to be the kind of leader who has a fiefdom and sets people to work upon the barricades? Or do you want to be the kind who makes the air smoother for them, gliding at the vertex of the V?

17

Does the leader lead by walking the course or by leading others onto the course?

It is hard to do one but not the other. Walking the course, and again walking the course, one begins to assimilate one's being into it, to become its strength and clarity, to add to its fragrance. To be that, and to be around others, draws them in to the stuff of the emptied self so that they cannot help but walk the course as well. And if they do not walk the course as well, the leader will not notice it anyway, because the scope of their actions and effects will shrink to a squiggle on the margin of the movement.

Try to lead, and you will arrive at nothing. Pursue the goal from the place of Nothing, and you will have always already led.

18

Set a skiff on a slow river, and you will be led. Board the Chinatown budget bus, and you will be brought. Lie flat upon the dumb earth, and you will be carried. Strap into the rocket, and you will be floated.

The Activist sets a skiff on unspeaking and is led; they board a bus in nonaction and are brought; they lie flat upon Nothing and are carried; they strap into the true goal and are floated.

If you want to know whom to follow, look for the one who is led.

You can always see them, in the loading bay by the dumpsters, carrying a key.

Master of
the Encampment

1

Shadowed and desolate without a set shape, always transforming without any constancy—isn't that just politics? Isn't that the way that left and right go floating all the way down day and night? To where could the spark of justice go—but also, how could it stay put? In this great sack of the universe, what home could it find to rejoin?

These are the sort of questions that the old practitioners of the course might have asked. Encampment Jo caught some wind of these and was ecstatic. She started telling ridiculous, gassy stories about these ideas and giving preposterous lectures that didn't have any discernible beginning or ending. She then just let loose and wouldn't be a part of the movement but also still wouldn't see things as one self-marginalized. Although she realized how enamored of shadows everyone was, and that it was simply not possible to talk with the encampment, she still just flooded the place with her theories, taking whatever was repeated from the ancient days as true, putting all sorts of speeches in the mouths of people who never said any such thing, and using any anecdote she could to get the word out. Though alone, she could sit herself down with a six-pack in a flower garden, toasting the moon and hanging out with the spirit of heaven and earth. She wasn't too proud to be just another object—but she definitely wouldn't adjust herself to the habits of everyone around her, going back to arguing about "right" and "wrong."

Frankly, her stories and her logic were all overgrown and disorganized, though in the end they're probably harmless. Her words were uneven and just downright odd, but there's still maybe something worth looking at in them. In any case, what follows in this section is a record of some of the things that Jo kept going on about. She liked going off to roam with Whatever-It-Is-That-Creates, but she also liked to make friends with anyone who stands outside of the back-and-forth and who never believed in any ending or beginning. If such readers could get to the root of what she said, it might be vast and expansive, like a great cypress beside a Confucian temple, inexhaustibly full of the kind of non-truth truth that came down from her originary sect. All I know is that it seems very dim and obscure, and I would have a hard time explaining any of it.

2

First, Jo said:

"There used to live a lonely fish named Swarm, who had built a house in the middle of the Arctic Ocean. I do not know exactly how large Swarm was, but he was at least eight light-years long from nose to tail. Swarm took it into his head to travel south through the Americas, so he leaped out of the ocean somewhere near Kugaaruk and transformed into a bird named Association. Association was considerably larger than he had been as the fish named Swarm, so you can imagine that he needed to fly quite high above the earth so that there would be enough air to hold him up as he flapped his wings. He began to fly south, wheeling in great swooping dives across the face of the continent, enjoying the feeling of starlight on his back, and acting totally at his ease, without much concern for what might have been going on below.

"As it happened, while Association was passing directly over the middle of the United States, there happened to be a young boy of incipient fascistic tendencies who had brought out a magnifying glass to an anthill in his backyard. The boy was enjoying an experiment he had heard about from his friends, focusing the rays of the sun on the ants to see if he could light them on fire. He had already blasted several, to his great satisfaction, and had high hopes that he might be able to get the entire ant nest to burst into flames, when suddenly the entire landscape darkened into an unexpected night, as lonely Association began passing in front of the sun. The boy was severely disappointed, but as he had no other method of lasering the ant colony, he took his magnifying glass and went back into his house.

"Three ants came up from their burrow, looked up, and saw Association blocking out the sun. At this point, they made very cutting remarks about him, saying that he was lost in a selfish pseudo-loftiness, unconcerned with on-the-ground organization, and completely hopeless for either organizing resistance or for making positive change. They posted a large number of viral hashtags about Association, exposing him to much online scorn.

"Eventually, Association flew out of range, leaving the United States nice and sunny again."

3

Then Jo said:

"In the real world, the world of objects, there is no object which is a 'this,' and no object that stands opposed to it as a 'that.' If one comes from a place of thatting things, then one will never see this; but if one comes from a place of knowledge, one can know. That is why, long ago, it was said, "Thats come from thisses, and thisses give rise to thats." Even in matters of life and death, one can only have 'life' when one has 'death,' and one can only get 'death' out of 'life.' So how much more obvious is it that 'logically correct' can only exist in the presence of 'logically incorrect,' and vice versa? And of course, one can only get 'right' when one has 'wrong,' and "wrong' can only exist once one has named a 'right.' Do not be so quick to go looking for a rope on a winter dawn; the branch might not bear the freight you intend.

"There are people who take the that as wrong and the this as right, only because there must also be people who take the this as wrong and the that as right. So long as there is a right and a wrong, the right and wrong will create a these people and a those people. Right cannot conquer wrong, nor can wrong conquer right. In human affairs, things must pass on to and replace each other, cycling in their turns. If you were to take all those people who love the wrong, and you were to put each and every one into an oven, but you left alive the categories of 'right' and 'wrong,' the word 'wrong' would by itself again reconstitute a movement.

"This is why the Activist does not try to win out over their enemies but tries to win out over the language that creates enemies. Only when the divisions of right and wrong evaporate into the wind can there be an end to the 'those' who try to repress our 'these.'"

4

Once, I asked Jo about how to get straight to the right principles of things.

Jo answered:

"Using a finger to point out the fingerlessness of fingers is not as good as using an unfinger to point out the fingerlessness of fingers. I know you want an index for what I indicate, but indexes are made for the indexical. If there never was indexicality, why do you keep demanding that I give you the finger and call it pointing out? The course only goes up to where the white clouds stop, there on the horizon."

5

Then Jo said, with tears soaking her blouse:

"I dreamed that I dreamed I was a butterfly, fluttering carefree and easy, following wherever my mind led me, and not knowing a thing about anyone named 'Jo.' Then, suddenly, I awoke, and I was just Jo again, fluttering carefree and easy as a haiku. I did not know if I was Jo who had dreamed of being a butterfly, or if I was a butterfly dreaming of being Jo. Now that I've awoken from that dream, I realize that once I had had names for 'Jo' and 'butterfly,' then there had to be a division between the two. No names, no division; no butterfly, no Jo. The real transformation is the end of transformation."

After that, she dried her tears and created a new passport for herself, on the authority of something called the "People's Republic of Butterflies." To my knowledge, she was never stopped at a border, even though she migrated twice yearly.

6

Then Jo said:

"During the Occupy movement, I once joined an encampment in my hometown to protest a bank with major investments in sweatshop conglomerates. In the camp, we had our own activist chef, a vegan caterer named Beau who agreed with our movement. The protest leader, Winnie, came to watch Beau cook one of our lunches: he had old 1990s music blaring, like Rollins and RATM, and his huge knife kept swooshing left and right with the beat, and singing madly beside the five willows where the food station was set up. He was a smiler with a knife: he would stand a row of carrots on end, and with a quick thwick-thwack they'd all be peeled and diced; he could throw a handful of soybeans into the air, move his cleaver through them like thunder, and they would fall back to the cutting board as cubes of freshly pressed tofu.

"Winnie was astonished at this miraculous skill and asked Beau how he had arrived at such heights of culinary mastery. Beau said, 'This is nothing but my love of the course, brought over into my skill set. When I started off as a chef-in-training, all that I could see were vegetables in need of chopping, and my knife was always dull because I was always hacking away at them. Then after a few years I began to see beyond the vegetables, to the leaf tissues, the root cortices, the mesophylls, the xylem and phloem, all the structured sheaves of fiber running this way and that. When I learned to see them, my hand could learn to feel them, and my cleaver could run along instead of across them. Now I do not hack, nor do I cut, but I wave my blade and the food deconstructs itself. Sometimes I heat and season it a bit, but there is nothing here that could be called mastery.'

"Winnie said, 'Amazing! After learning this from you, Beau, I know how to take care of things.' At that point she borrowed his cleaver, swooshed it through the air at the bank, and the bank came apart, falling in great concrete and marble chunks around the street."

7

Then Jo said:

"Once upon a time, the apostle Peter came to see Jesus and said, 'Jesus, I've decided that it's time I left you and traveled to the United States.'

"Jesus said, 'Why would you go to that shithole country?'

"Peter said, 'The rulers of the United States have become ridiculous users of their own strength, throwing away lives for fun, not even making much of the fate of the country, and generally acting like jackasses for no reason other than to prove that they can. I once heard you say, "They that are whole have no need of the physician, but they that are sick." Since no one is as sick as the Americans, I thought I ought to go help them.'

"Jesus said, 'Oh, my god, Peter, you really missed the point. When you set out along the course, you need to follow it, not start taking on all these side quests. When your side quests multiply, you will get confused; when you get confused, you will get depressed; and once you're depressed, there won't be any saving you.

"'You need to be grounded before you can engage. I know that you are focused upon peace and justice. But if you carry peace and justice to a nation founded upon the sacred principle of replying to "peace" and "justice" with "deez nuts," whom will you save? You are just becoming what they have hoped to create: foils for their bummillinery. When those who create conflict and demand conflict go roaming around cable news daring you to stand up for peace and justice, would you take the bait?'

"Peter said, 'What if I were careful to be peaceful in my calls for peace, and just in my calls for justice, showing that my words were substantial and, therefore, preventing any kind of misrepresentation in social media clips?'

"Jesus said, 'How could that help? That would make things even worse. If you raised the banner of oppositional language but lacked even the putrid mind of those used to violence and confrontation, then you would just be inciting a celebratory self-annihilation. There's self-sacrifice for the cause, and then there's scrambling to be the first one under the front wheel of the steam engine.'

"Peter asked, 'If the United States is really a lost cause, and I shouldn't go there, then what should I be doing?'

"Jesus said, 'I didn't say the United States was a lost cause. You can help the Americans by going on a hunger strike.'

"Peter said, 'But Jesus, I am already on a hunger strike! For the last month, I have had nothing to eat at all, and nothing to drink except water, and a cup of clear broth once per day. Doesn't that count?'

"Jesus said, 'For fuck's sake, Peter, that's a religious fast or maybe a fad diet. What I'm talking about is a hunger strike of the mind.'

"Peter said, 'What is a hunger strike of the mind?'

"Jesus said, 'It's when you stop consuming through the eyes and the ears, ending your mind's swallowing of symbols, growing inhuman as a hawk's cry, and letting your hunger for words consume itself until you have entered into pure awareness without input. This desolation is the hunger strike of the mind.'

"Peter thought about this for a few minutes and then said, 'When I've been so busy trying to make change in the world, and failing, I've always had the strongest sense of myself as a real person named "Peter" who is trying to accomplish something. But very occasionally, when I've forgotten about being Peter for a bit, I've started to get something done. Then I can feel my mind following along with the wild geese flying south. Is that what you mean by "desolation"?'

"Jesus said, 'Yup, that's it! When you stop acknowledging your name, society no longer has a box in which to place you. Then you can be free of the clash of activist and reactionary and start to take real action. You can slip through the interstices of social structures, squirm away from any grabbing representation, homing in on the divine wherever you are and making change wherever you are not. This is all the Law and the Prophets.'"

8

Then Jo said:

"Once, during the Cultural Revolution, there was a team of sent-down youth assigned to a forestry team in the northeast, near the North Korean border. They became very good at clear-cutting the wooded hills and bringing the trees down past camp to where they could be shipped off to the lumber mills. From there, the trees could be processed into all kinds of boards, converted from their original natures into something that could be useful to the eternal revolution.

"One day, surprisingly far up the side of a mountain in the Changbai range, they discovered a monstrous ash tree. When they climbed up to the base of the tree, it loomed into the size of a universe, twisting in massive braids of wood down into the rooted earth and up into the branching heavens, reaching out from the earth across all of the nine realms. It sang, high and aloof: its sources in the tips of its roots were buried and could not be seen, nor could the extremities of its branches, thinning out into filaments that reached beyond the clouds. What could be seen was the giant buckling of its trunk in bulges, each scale upon its bark the size of one of the great boulders of scree that lay nearby upon the mountain's upper flanks.

"When the students had spent time marveling at the tree and inspecting it, their team leader, a boy named Hong, suddenly cried out, 'This is fantastic—what a tree! Let us immediately chop it down and bring it to the mills. Once we can turn this miracle into boards, it can satisfy any need that the revolution might have for wood! With this wood, we would bring communism to the whole earth within a year.'

"The students' local guide, a crusty mountain man named Woodsman Xu, replied, 'I'm sorry, but that tree isn't good for anything. See how gnarled and knotted it is? It has followed its own nature, become all twisted and warped, and that is why it has lived so long and grown so large. If you tried to turn it into timber, the boards would bend and snap. Better to focus on cutting down and processing all those straight, strong, young trees that want to be useful; they are the ones that would. This useless old thing can only be what it is; let the grasses and the trees keep their original minds.'"

9

Then Jo said:

"I have heard a story about a Vietnam protest march in which one of the protestors was a veteran named Sam who had lost both of his arms at Hué, bit by a cartridge with fine zinc teeth. The march organizer, Will, had previously stipulated that every single person who joined the march must be willing and able to carry a placard: he had wanted the cameras to capture a great rushing sea of protest slogans. So, Will said to Sam, 'I'm very sorry about this, but you can't follow the rules for this march, so you are not allowed to join.' The person who told me this story, Simon, said he thought that maybe Will was suspicious of Sam as a vet and thought perhaps that he had sacrificed his arms on purpose to be able to foul up the march.

"Simon also told me that he had argued with Will, trying to stand up for Sam. He said to Will, 'Why do you want my friend to hold up a sign? Can't you see that he is himself the best sign we could ever want? You should carry him on your shoulders if you want us to really be sending a message.'

"Sam did not seem happy at this suggestion, but he did not show any indication of what he was thinking. Instead, he walked away, and all that Simon could tell me was that he thinks Sam spent most of the rest of the war in a cabin somewhere in West Virginia, going home to lie down on the corner of the mountains. Will got his way with the march, but it did not end the war. When the war did end several years later, it was Sam's doing."

10

Once, I startled Jo while she was pacing lazily, holding a palm-leaf sutra and muttering. I asked her for a story, and she told me the following:

"One time, Jen went to Crazy J to ask her how to run an encampment. Crazy J started by asking Jen, 'What did Earl tell you about it?' Jen replied, 'He said that it is important to set up clear rules and standards, making sure that everyone knew the code of conduct, both to preserve internal consensus and unity of purpose, and to present a united front to the media and other external forces to maximize impact. Moreover, this form of standards-based leadership requires the dedication of the encampment leader; only when rules are based in his strong will will they become efficacious.'

"Crazy J said, 'What bullshit! Asking a leader to enact a code of conduct is like sending a mountain by air freight on Gnat Express. It's a simple question of weight ratios. Can a protest leader even create a perfect set of standards that would govern her own behavior, let alone pour forth a set of standards that would govern the camp? On the contrary, she ought to use whatever will she has to duck out of the way of codes and regulations. Smart fish dive below the reach of nets, and smart birds fly off when the shooting starts. Why wouldn't an activist try to escape entrapment? Why would she build more traps for herself?'"

When she had finished the story, Jo picked up her leaf again, gave me a weirdly piercing look, and said, "Try your best to cross over away from all that, the way plum or willow branches might try to cross a river in spring."

11

Then Jo said:

"Once upon a time, there was a great emperor of the Southern Seas, named 'Sound.' And there was a great emperor of the Northern Seas, named 'Din.' But the greatest emperor of them all was the emperor of the central lands, and their name was 'Primordial Mess.'

"Now, one day, Sound and Din had both come to visit Primordial Mess in their central kingdom, and when they arrived, they were trumpeted in with fanfare and a universal hubbub wild. Primordial Mess was an incredibly warm and gracious host, providing the two visiting royals with all that a person of nobility could wish for: dazzling spectacles, entrancing music, and the richest of cuisines at every meal. The only problem was that their host seemed to be pure substance, with no qualities adhering to them. It was very disconcerting.

"Sound and Din took to discussing how they could repay this hospitality. Sound said to Din, 'Men all have seven gates in our heads by which we can perceive, enjoy, assess, and order life. Yet our gracious host has none; they cannot even enjoy these spectacles, music, and cuisines which they have so generously provided us.' And Din said to Sound, 'Yes, let us bore seven holes in their head. Then, not only will they be able to enjoy life, they will also be able to direct and bring order to their kingdom, just like we bring order to ours.'

"So, filled with gratitude, Sound and Din took a golden auger, and each day they bored one hole in the head of Primordial Mess: eyes, ears, nostrils, and mouth. After a week, Primordial Mess sighed softly from their new mouth and died. Without an emperor, the people of the central lands were forced to learn politics."

12

Once, Jo and I sat together in a cabin, in a winter, in a forest where no zither played, and no one felt close. Staring at the cold lamp, she thought of her former life. Then Jo said:

"I joined the women's march wearing my own authentic pink pussy hat and carrying a sign saying, 'MY BODY MY CHOICE.' Then the Trump courts took away my choice.

"Taking my choice, they did not take my body. And the body regenerates choice spontaneously—even when shackled by irons. Shackled only by the word and the words called 'Law,' how could I not continue to choose?

"I had sex when I wanted.

"I used contraception when I wanted.

"I moved across state and national borders when I wanted.

"I slit the throats of my would-be rapists when I wanted and saw their stupid fisheyes glaze over as they chose to flap around in their own blood.

"Animals can be caged, but they cannot be socialized into a law that falsifies their biology. Knowing this, they live their lives rather than joining movements."

We faced each other, and I forgot how to speak. It was then in the cold lamplight that I noticed the small red letter "B" tattooed proudly on the inside of her left wrist.

13

Then Jo said:

"Every unhappy presidency is unhappy in its own way.

"George Bush was once on one of his brush-clearing vacations on his Texas ranch. He got out his chainsaw and safety goggles, media scrum following along behind the pickup with the presidential seal. He had determined to cut a path through the scrub on the west pasture for easy access to a media-appropriate creek in which men of the people seem to like to fish.

"He went back and forth with his chainsaw, cutting in straight lines from the truck ruts down to the creek bank but could not manage to clear even the narrowest path. As he cut away brush, the straight lines seemed to become winding, and the branches that were sawn off blocked the way forward. It did not seem that new branches magically sprang up to replace the ones cut, only that infinite cuts could be made without diminishing the amount of remaining brush. After a few hours, the straight-line path that the president had tried to cut was not only not clear, it was a straight-line mess of cut but unclearable branches and brambles. Even the burly Secret Service men in their camouflage suits could not push their way down to the water.

"Then the president noticed one of his ranch hands standing by who had been assigned to accompany the sawing party but not to interfere unless he was directly asked for assistance. He was a man born to the scrublands whom the president always called 'Jorge,' though I do not know his real name.

"'Jorge,' said the president, 'do you see a way through this?'

"'Yes, Mr. President. The problem is that you have tried to cut the straight and have found the crooked. But that is not the way that the brush grows, so it is not the way that you can stop it from growing. You should have tried to cut crooked so that you could go straight. Then not even a cut is needed.'

"And with that the hand ducked behind a bush for just a minute or two. With a rustle in the reeds, there returned the ranch hand, and he waved to the president and the entourage to follow. He seemed to duck and weave through the mess of thorns, but when the followers caught up with him, they could see that he had indeed found a clear, wide path down to the water. Looking forward and looking back, while on the path, it could be seen to be both level and direct, as if the plants had simply chosen not to grow there. Nothing was cut, and nothing was unnatural, but the path went exactly where they wanted to go.

"When they reached the river, the president said, 'Well, heck, Jorge, you're a real bushmaster. I've never seen such a straight shooter as you. Instead of having you cut through this mess out on my ranch, I should bring you to Washington to cut through all the red tape!'

"The laborer said, 'Please spare me, Mr. President, and don't hire me into your cabinet! Here on the land I know the way things grow and see into the movement of living things toward the sun. They react according to their nature, and when I am with them, I am free to follow my own nature as well. Out here, I am very good at nourishing the grand airs within me. But the tangles you speak of are not from anything natural; they are patterns made of nothing and yet constructed into iron tangles. I do not know if they would be worth cutting or not; I only know that I would be cut by them. I do not value my life so little as to try to accomplish something.'"

14

When the hair at her temples was already thinning and flecked with white, Jo said:

"Being in opposition to another requires an other, but it also requires 'opposition' as a known and named force. Without 'opposition' there is no opposition. Ditch the word, and you cannot oppose anyone else, but they can also not oppose you, nor can they oppose what you're fighting for. There never was a dragon for you to tame, just an empty pool and a temple bell.

"Some species do not know how to form parties, movements, and factions, but hominids do. Chimps form power structures without the word 'opposition,' but they have the word within the word, and this is enough for confusion. We have the words to contain our words, so usually if we can get rid of our words, that will suffice to get rid of the words also. Remember, you cannot step into the same stream of consciousness twice.

"Systems of difference structure systems of indifference. Deconstruct these, and those will deconstruct themselves."

15

Then Jo said:

"A hawk circled the sky over the woodlands, looking downward for prey. Colors were quiet within the deep pines, but it saw a rustling in the grass that fit the exact pattern of a scampering vole. In fact, it saw a tuft of gray that was exactly vole sized. So, it dove, coming straight from the direction of the blinding sun, falling with wings tucked to gain insuperable speed.

"When the hawk was only a few yards from the ground, it realized that the tuft of gray was not a vole but a large adult male wolf. Unable to check its own speed, the hawk flew right into the maw of the wolf and was eaten.

"Having been eaten, the hawk was not able to pass on to the general hawk community an important lesson about perspective, which would have been useful."

16

Like an eastern sea giving birth to a bright moon, Jo said:

"There was a protest leader who was enamored of the simplicity of mathematics and wanted to have clear boundaries between those who were allies and those who were enemies. Therefore, in setting up fencing around his encampment, he mapped out the space along two axes and then defined a function in terms of the two variables that specified the boundaries of the encampment at each point.

"And so, the protestors under his direction dutifully began calculating and marking out the path of the encampment enclosure fencing. However, they had not gotten very far into the work when they realized that the edge of the fencing would have to be very rough—in fact, infinitely rough. One protestor would try to bend the fence by a tiny amount to accommodate the calculated boundary, and then the other would rightly point out that the bend would need another bend to be closer to correct. Each bend required another, smaller bend, and those bends required smaller bends again. Unable to match the reality of the material world to the clarity of the predicted values of the boundaries, the camp fell into argument over proper and improper approximations, and the narrower the scope of the argument, the more vicious the fighting became. In one bulbous protrusion, an argument over the modeling of the boundary within a single square millimeter resulted in multiple stabbings and four deaths.

"The Activist does not believe in clarifying, and this is why he does not build boundaries. Once, a long time ago, a king of the state of Chu lost his great Ravenscaw Bow while hunting. His attendants offered to search for it, but the king said, 'A king of Chu lost it, and a person of Chu will find it. Why bother looking?' When Confucius heard of it, he shook his head and said, 'The king should have said, "A king lost it, and a person will find it." Who cares about Chu?' Then Laozi heard what Confucius had said, and he said, 'Actually, the king should have said, "Something lost it, and something has already found it." Who cares about people?'"

17

It was the middle of the night, and Jo could not sleep. She sat up and played her resounding zither as her thin curtains shone through with bright moonlight. Then she wrote the following in her journal:

"It is not that I do not understand the value of thinking and acting tactically on the way to my goal. It is that you do not understand that you are taught by tactics to pursue the wrong goal.

"A chess grandmaster named Honed was visiting Manhattan. He had heard of an unnamed, shabby old man playing chess in Central Park who would lay down his white hairs each night beneath the pines and the clouds. This man may have been homeless, and no one knew his name, but the regular park players called him Hum because he was always saying 'hmm' while sitting at the chess tables. Honed had heard that Hum had never lost a match, so he was eager to find him and play against him. In preparation, Honed was expecting a brilliant form of unorthodox park-playing style, so he reviewed all his books of notes on the most unconventional tactics and most famously surprising games from tournament play. Honed found Hum and sat down across from him; he then opened with a simple e4, waiting to see where his brilliant, unorthodox opponent might take the game.

"At this point, Hum grabbed Honed's backpack and ran out of the park, remaining undefeated.

"By devoting oneself to tactics, one loses sight of strategy; by devoting oneself to strategy, one loses sight of the world. The incense could burn forever behind royal curtains, but it's only lit when there's a concubine to play the flute. If I were to pursue my well-defined political goal by making lists of activism dos and don'ts, I would have an orderly movement but would not advance toward my goal. If I were to pursue my well-defined political goal by organizing a continent-wide multichannel campaign involving millions, I would advance toward my goal but would increase continent-wide stress, anger, depression, and misery vastly in excess of the good of my goal. And on the way to that well-planned misery, I would have converted my being into a mechanical mind.

"This is why I do not plan to effect change efficiently upon others. I change, and I invite the others along."

18

Then Jo said:

"Confucius said, 'The ancients said, "Desire is structured like a language." This is why they learned not to speak. To speak is to call forth one word after another, and even after one has stopped speaking, the echoes of what could have been said, and what still could be said, reverberate until the speaking resumes. One cannot follow the chain to the end; one can only break it.'

"Desire is also a chain: goal follows goal within a structure of possible goals, and attainment only calls forth the sum total of unattained goals. To cut off desire does not mean to cut off the body's desires of sex, taste, and thrill. It does not mean to cut off the spirit's desires of love, home, and happiness. To cut off those desires and to leave the burning desire for extinguishing the self in nirvana is not to extinguish the self; it is to burn with desire.

Let the white sun lean against the nearest mountain, then let it be swallowed up in an afterglow and the afterglow in darkness.

"Recognizing the structure of desire should change political desire. Do not psycho hack yourself. It is not just a mistake for your health; it is a mistake for justice to say that you can sacrifice yourself on the wheel of desire if by doing so you can attain end after end. Giving yourself over to political desire leads you to mistake the attainable for the end and to mistake the protestable for the attainable. No one loves a conflict junkie, even those who succeed in thinking themselves 'strident.'

"The grackle ate the finch, and the hawk ate the grackle. Some feathers were scattered around the river valley, and no one flew."

19

Jo lived in a downtown apartment, but she never heard traffic or bustle. I asked her once how she accomplished this, and she told me, "My mind goes far off into the wilds, and the apartment follows along." Then she told me the following story:

"A stone carver was working near the city gates of old Chang'an whom all the glitterati called Zippy the Mason. He was particularly sought after as a carver of stone steles, especially memorial steles for the dead. His chisel was swift and sure and could inscribe a block of stone like a chopstick tracing curves through tofu. Whenever one of the elite poets at the court was asked to write a praise of some recently deceased noble, they all required that Zippy be hired to transfer the calligraphy onto the stone, because only he was thought trustworthy enough to replicate the brushstrokes. Not only could he do so stroke for stroke, but he did it thought for thought and qi for qi. All his steles for the dead were as fresh as life.

"One day, another mason named Slips-the-Knot came to Zippy to try to recruit him into a new masons' guild that he was trying to organize. Slips-the-Knot said to Zippy, 'You think that your strength as a mason is in your right arm, but your only real strength is in unity with the rest of us. We all know that you are the most favored for carving work by all the richest and the most powerful of the land, but do not think that your rich and powerful patrons have your interests at heart. They see you as a mere workman, not an artist: they think you derive your glory from their own hands, and they only prefer you because they think that you are the least-bad of us. That is why you are asked to do the delicate chisel work while the rest of us build walls and bridges. But when you are too old to hold your chisel without a quiver and can neither carve calligraphy nor cut heavy blocks for walls, your lords and grandees will not give you a pension. Join with us, and we will sell our labor only when we are all fed and kept well.'

"Zippy said, 'That is not the way to make change. I am making change just as I am.'

"Slips-the-Knot got very angry, and shouted, 'How are you making change? You are making the opposite of change. The words that you literally carve into stone are the ideology of the privileged class! You turn their aestheticized privilege into giant monoliths to sit upon the landscape, weighing down the empire with the words of authority. This is not change; this is stolidity.'

"Zippy pointed to the stele he was in the middle of carving. 'This stone seems firm and everlasting, but it is like a sheet of ice that flows away in the spring. The stele I am carving today is a replacement for the Stele in Memoriam of Marquis Wan of Dripdropton. The old one was carved by me only twenty years ago, but it has already been worn down to illegibility by the constant flow of scholars coming to take charcoal rubbings of the elegy, so prized it was as a literary and calligraphic masterpiece. That which stands out calls out for its own effacement.

"'Knowing that the stone is made of water, I have been able to shape it to my liking. Shaping the stone to my liking, I have amazed the literati. Having amazed the literati, I built my trade into a sign of status. Having built my trade into a sign of status, I command high fees. Commanding high fees, I extract wealth at will from the great lords of the realm. They indeed consider me a workman and not an artist. The mosquito considers me a juice box and not a constellation of mind. But when do the great care about the delusions of the small? I leave the great lords their delusions, and I extract their strings of coins. I bloom to myself and have no master.

"'All in the universe is in unending transformation. Who makes the transformation? This is a current one does not stop but can divert. Nowadays people think that the great Sage-King Yu transformed the world, but the ancients knew that Yu was transformed by his subjects. You have said that I am inscribing the ideology of the ruling classes into the unchangeable permanence of stone. I feel sorry that you are so slow to catch on! I am using the illusory permanence of stone to transform the ideology of the ruling classes. Believing that they can entrust their calligraphy to me to transform into stone, they are led to commission these decorations for their own transformation into bone. Everywhere along the highways they erect these steles, announcing their own mortality. I transform their culture into a culture of self-transformation: after this, who will take them seriously?

"'On the other hand, if I were to join your guild, and we were to restrict the supply of our labor, demanding higher rates, and nice titles, and a pension plan, we would be raising the cost and the obnoxiousness of masonry. The grandees would tire of stone and would turn to silk. Lacking the stuff of memorials, they would not memorialize but would go back to gambling and drinking games and shut the gates of ideology to all of us.'

"Slips-the-Knot scoffed, 'I see. You are just one of those lickspittles who opposes any kind of collective action.'

"Zippy replied, 'Collective action is fine, but it cannot measure up to collective inaction. Instead of me joining your guild, your guild should join me. Then we would repave the skies with stones finer than what Nü Wa used.'"

20

Then Jo said:

"Have you heard the story called 'Three in the Morning'?

"A Di's Combo Burger franchise owner had a problem with his employees, who hated their shift schedule. He required them to work three hours in the morning, leave, and then come back to work four hours at night. This created havoc for all of them, interfering with their schedules for work or school, making family life and childcare impossible, and causing them to spend twice as much time commuting every day.

"One day, the employees got sick of it. From the high-school students to the retirees, they all got together and demanded a meeting with the owner. They complained to him of the impossibility of working three hours in the morning and then four at night. So, the owner gave in and yielded to their demands. The next week he changed the shift schedules so that all the workers had to work four hours in the morning and three at night. And all the employees were delighted and had a victory party to celebrate their progress in ameliorating their work conditions.

"At another Di's Combo Burger franchise in the same city, a different owner had set the same schedule for his employees. (This was recommended by Di's Combo Burger executives at the annual franchisee workshop, once they had collected all phones and other recording devices.) This owner was much fiercer and more dominating, so his employees did not dare band together to ask for better shift schedules. Instead, they each just worked for a few weeks, until they couldn't take it anymore, and then they quit, one at a time. There was no collaboration, no unity, and no victory party. Each former employee found their way somewhere else. And after six months of constant employee turnover, this second owner started offering unified regular nine-to-five shifts so that he could keep his Di's Combo Burger open."

21

Then Jo said:

"Affairs of this world are like a boat upon the waves. You can see the wave as it crests but cannot see the wave as it is gestating. You can see the fight as it bursts against batons and riot shields, but you cannot see the fight within its seed.

"Organization, structure, positions and roles—those are only the seed coat, the outer shiny surface of the fight to be. They are not the fight itself.

"Below that is the ideology, the endosperm that nourishes—but this is only what allows the fight to be fueled and to grow out of the seed and into itself. But this is also not the fight itself.

"Within that are the people waiting to become the fight: one is a cotyledon, one a hypocotyl, and one a radicle, each waiting their turn in different ways, to become the leaf, stem, and root of the fight. These are us, in the bodies where we live, but we are also not the fight.

"The fight is in the aerenchyma, the empty spaces in the seed that let it float through water or air to the places it might germinate, light as a boat whose oars could startle a goose. Only with emptiness can the seed travel far enough to shape the land, like a lone tumbleweed on a thousand-mile trek. Holding tightly onto that emptiness, the rest might not even be needed."

22

Then Jo said:

"You have heard it said, 'Follow the void to its end, and hoard silence.'

"But I say to you, do not hoard the silence itself, but hoard the rationality made plain in the silence. Only when you hoard the rationality in the silence can you overturn the state organs of repression. You cannot see the ancients behind you, nor the people of the future in front, but you can see clearly who and where you are if you concentrate.

"There are those who meditate and seek to strip themselves of cognition. They cut off the world to focus on a mantra or upon the breath. They hope to graduate from the focus on the breath to the focus on nothing at all, and from the focus on nothing to non-focus and non-cognition. Perhaps some achieve this, but this is not what I call being natural, or spiritual, or an Activist.

"We are cognitive engines. Those who meditate wrongly, trying to blank themselves, can never return to the bare fact of nature: it is the nature of a mind to think. This is just the quietest illusion. The real silence of the Activist is the silence that strips away all illusions and confronts the bare facts of what exists and what does not. Seeing without illusion is the precondition for change.

"When Laozi was working as an archivist in the royal records hall in the Zhou dynasty palace, Confucius came to see him and asked for his help in finding records relating to ancient ritual practice. Laozi did not answer but kept reading through some rolls of bamboo-strip books. Confucius repeated his request several times, but Laozi did not say a word, nor did he acknowledge that Confucius was even in the same room. Therefore, Confucius said at last, 'Ah, I understand. The ritual of the ancients was to see nothing, say nothing, and know nothing. I will go back to Lu and teach this to my students.'

"Laozi had not noticed that Confucius had come, had not noticed him speaking, and did not notice his departure. Laozi was simply very good at concentrating, like a gull hanging between heaven and earth."

23

Then Jo said:

"Appendixes are vestigial organs. They must have had some digestive function for prehominids, but now they just sit around waiting to get infected. It's an excrescence that we really ought to evolve beyond at some point. They come out of our genetic legacy but are not in harmony with the selves that we are as humans now.

"Tumors are worse than vestigial organs; they come from cells that break out of the mold, wanting to live their best YOLO lives, and hell with the genetic rules that say when and where they get to grow. Cut them out, and they just send cells out to go be bad boys everywhere else in the body. And then they kill the whole being. This is the natural organism developing naturally against its own nature.

"Ideology is a natural outgrowth of the body politic, but a natural addition over and against nature that kills the nature. Our movement leaders tell us that we cannot see clearly without ideology; this is like praising the 8K hi-res pixel count on new VR goggles. Cut out the excrescence to live longer; remove the blinders to see farther."

24

Then Jo said:

"You have heard it said, 'The constant course never does anything, and so there is nothing it cannot do.'

"But I tell you that the course does nothing because it is a certain kind of nothing, and it can achieve everything because it is that certain kind of nothing.

"The ghostly forms of furniture did not exist in the mind of God before the world; we can abstract the form of a bed from real beds through repeated cognitive exposure to the things we lie down on. We can see the patterns of dunes along the windy shorelines, of birds entranced into murmurations, of the distribution of tree species in a maturing forest, of a green haze melting into nothingness. And we can see the forms by which movements coalesce, grow, protest, achieve goals, and die away. None of these forms and patterns exist in God. They exist only as forms and patterns, and they act everywhere without acting, accomplishing everything while imbued in the substance of the world as it is.

"A human is not a nothing; a human is a being. A human has the course running through them, without being the course. To follow the course as a human is not to make oneself into nothing, any more than it is to make oneself into everything. To follow the course is to be what one is, and to act without acting is to see clearly the patterns of the world as it is and to walk along them."

25

Someone had locked Jo in an attic. When I let her out, she said:

"Cesar Millan trains dogs according to the nature of dogs, which need exercise and discipline before affection. Bad doggies become good doggies under his touch because they yearn in the recesses of their atavistic wolf hearts for a pack leader.

"Jackson Galaxy trains cats according to the nature of cats, which need exercise and territorial control before affection. Bad kitties become good kitties under his touch because they yearn in the recesses of their primordial lion hearts for an open hunting ground upon the savannah.

"Our protest leaders have trained us according to the needs of the ideology, not according to our nature as humans. As humans, we need physical and social sustenance before we need political victory; but we have been taught to sacrifice our health and our relationships in the service of political victory. Under their touch, we started as good people and have become malfunctioning people with good ideals. Turning away from one's evolved nature as a human in the service of a goal is not an act of heroism. It dwarfs state repression as the leading cause of death among activists: hacking our own endocrine systems to revolt against what we are, we can only wither and sicken."

26

Then someone interrupted Jo:

"I keep hearing you attack ideology, as if you are free of ideology! We all live the ideology of justified resistance, and you want us to adopt your ideology of mystical do-nothingism. You can pretend that your ridiculous ideas are somehow not the lickspittle's self-adjustment to the interests of the ruling class. But you can't pretend that they aren't an ideology! There is no option to be nonideological; the question is: what ideology and whose interest does it serve?"

Jo sighed and paused, shaking her head. She then spoke a little too loudly, with the high-pitched lisp that people employ when talking to their babies or their kittens: "If I were the kind of person who lived within an ideology, I would be able to draw all kinds of fine distinctions between 'ideologies,' 'ideas,' 'concepts,' 'doctrines,' 'theories,' 'judgments,' 'cognitive habits,' 'opinions,' 'delusions,' 'dreams,' 'slam poetry,' and 'anxious Tourette's interjections shouted at the bus stop as imprecatory prayers against half-remembered moments of ancient shame.' I would have thought you would be able to, too. But because neither of us can, let me explain it this way.

"When I was a teenager, I starved myself to be thin. My ideal of beauty was Buchenwald-survivor chic. Then I went online, learned the words 'anorexia' and 'body dysmorphic disorder,' and had my eyes opened to the fact that not only was I harming myself but also reinforcing patriarchal modes of control over female bodies through the ideology of fashionable emaciation. To undo the damage I had done to peers by reinforcing that model, I tried to liberate them by eating everything possible and celebrating my weight gains. It was difficult to consume so much without participating in the systems of industrial agriculture, but eventually I was able to raise my weight from 7.5 pounds to 75,000 pounds. At that point, I was full of body positivity and quite proud to be able to share my progress on social media, subverting the patriarchy. But my success in following the new program had mobilized me to immobility, and I was stuck in a cocoon of myself, eventually unable even to type.

"No longer able to liberate, I learned gradually to shrink back from my ideology. I did not renounce it and still have not renounced it: renunciation of an ideology is, indeed, another ideology. But I stopped feeding it, and it stopped growing into me. I learned to see things as they were. There was no norm for my body, thin or fat, to which it could aspire. There was no 'should' about food, only foods and effects. There was no one kind of hunger in myself but a vast array of deficiencies, desires, habits, and addictions. I did not go on any diet program, nor any political program, but learned to see clearly whether my body required a celery stalk, a family pack of Cheez Productz, or a pint of dew harvested from dawn asphodels in the Cyclades. I think I have lost weight, and I must be somewhere between 7.5 and 75,000 pounds, but I do not measure myself anymore. By seeing myself as I am, and objects as they are, I have become a self who can finally again act in the world."

27

Then Jo said:

"One thing that ideologues do understand is the uselessness of suitcase locks.

"When your suitcase has a combination lock, or a tiny miniature padlock to thread through the zipper eyelets, you can keep the ticket-counter agent from opening it right in front of you. But if the suitcase gets properly checked and sent on along, anyone can walk up to the luggage carousel, pick up your suitcase and leave with it, if they get there before you. Tiny, picayune barriers to fiddling won't stop a bold bandit who is willing to carry off everything at once.

"Even the most addled Agitator knows that the state is a suitcase, and its laws are like flimsy suitcase locks. Anyone who attempts to snap off the lock while playing by the rules of the lock will get caught: this is why the sad-sack moron who tries to rob a bank by showing up at the teller window with a gun will definitely, certainly be caught. But the great man will simply carry off the entire bank without a second thought: the CEO gooses the numbers, robs the bank by dictating his own compensation package to the board, and walks out the door with hundreds of millions. Alexander cut open a knot and absconded with Persia. No law can stop the grand theft because laws are designed to enable the grand theft.

"Coup leaders are the most magnificent grand-scale thieves of all, because they steal the state itself. Election laws are suitcase combination locks; electioneering norms are suitcase zipper mini padlocks. There are those who try to break the rules by fiddling with the delicate little machinery of elections, and they win or lose, serve a term or get hounded out under the power of the law: either way, they are small thieves. The grand thief is the one who ignores all these trifling barriers, walks up to the luggage carousel, and carries off the nation-state entire and whole. Grand thieves cannot be caught by the law because they have become the lawgivers. Rules are the tools of the grand thieves.

"What the Activist knows is that the encampment leader is a tiny grand thief, because the encampment is a tiny state. Rules are what make a lawn into a fiefdom. The rules are promulgated in language that honors the high, noble purpose of the political end goal and directs scrutiny toward the goal and away from the rule maker. That is what laws always do; it is their purpose. In fact, the function of the encampment rules is to prolong striving toward the goal while preventing its achievement. Only then can the encampment leader still have the fulfillment of an encampment in which to swaddle themself.

"Once, Tony the Scourge Lombardo came to Al Capone and asked, 'Does the Chicago Outfit also have a Course?' Al Capone answered, 'Of course we do! How else are we gonna bootleg? When we bring beer across from Windsor to Detroit, that's the

Smart Course. When we buy rye in Moose Jaw and tunnel it under the border, that's the Righteous Course. And when we just float the hooch right down Lake Michigan, that's the Course of Cultural Resistance. Any way we go, we are following the right Course—our tommy guns make sure of that!

"'Every day of my life I thank God for Prohibition! Without Prohibition, there would be no money to be made. I hope someday they ban food and water—we will be able to take the whole world. But if they repeal the laws, then we will be repealed, too. If nothing is prohibited, then no one will be dissatisfied, and all will return to the great peace of profitlessness. That would be boring—no jazz, no girls, and no Miami Beach parties. What's good for us is that the preachers and the temperance broads and all the other righteous progressives keep doubling down on more laws and more rules. If they keep it up, then I'm going to be president someday!

"'Tony, since you're my consigliere, I'll tell you a story I ain't never told nobody. Once upon a time in China, there was this wise guy named Zhuang who spent a lot of time studying philosophy, all kinds of bull about what makes hard shit hard and white shit white, what makes this this and that that. But then one day the wise guy got wise, and he figured out that all the college man stuff didn't go nowhere. You could invent a better mousetrap, but then the mice start hiding in the walls. You can invent a better fishhook, and then the fish just learn to cool their heels at the bottom of the lake. In other words, all the genius and the effort just set a new point for the homeostasis, see? That homeostasis is where the Outfit makes our money; never forget that. So, I couldn't have this Zhuang guy getting people wise. So, I got Frank Nitti to go over and put the hit on him; he sent word back that it was done on Valentine's Day. We didn't get Bugs Moran, but at least we got that lunkhead.'"

28

When Jo's hair went white, she said that it was only the hair that urged her to age. Then she told me:

"The failure of a political movement begins in the glands.

"Conflict as a way of life pumps anxiety and juices cortisol. Juiced cortisol packs the liver full of glucose and confuses melatonin levels. Confused melatonin levels leave no time for REM sleep. Missing REM sleep jacks up ghrelin and slashes leptin, making the mouth and mind ravenous. The conflict-based movement, therefore, leaves us anxious, tired, angry, and craving carbs right in the midst of our action.

"Can the best way to the goal be seen by someone who is anxious, tired, angry, and craving carbs? Or by someone who is calm, well-rested, rational, and craving justice? Put your movement in order to put your body in order; put your body in order to put your mind in order; put your mind in order to put the world in order. Unless you can do this, your movement will be a collection of cold boulders, filling an empty forest.

"Abbie Hoffman had been famous for years as the Emperor of the Yippies when he heard of a retreat being led by Master Shunryu Suzuki at the Tassajara Zen monastery. He came to the mountain to see the Master, and asked, 'Is there a Zen method to improve my prank-based protest? I want to use the Magic of the Eternal East to confuse the media lapdogs of the industrial capitalist state and make it rain down peace and cash on all the proletariat of this nation.' The Master replied, 'Peace and cash? You have only made it rain nonsense and anger. Under your reign of chaos, the war expands, the assassinations proliferate, the people lose their savings, and the planet begins a march to catastrophe.'

"Following this meeting, Abbie Hoffman was arrested for trying to change the White House into a jelly doughnut, and he spent three months in solitary confinement, meditating on a straw mat. When he was released, he came again to Master Suzuki and said, 'Since I have failed at governing my movement, may I ask about governing my own self?'

"The master replied, 'Now that's the right question. It's like this: your Buddha-nature is not your body, but it is also not not your body. Eliminate trips, traps, and techniques to allow your five senses to fast and detox. Stop the scheming and feeding the media, and you will allow all that is not mystery and quiet to flow out of your mind, and dissipate, and you will be left in a state where you can begin to see the Buddha-nature. In what is dark, you will find the lovely rich umami of the inexhaustible mind; and in what is light, you will find the understated honey of the undiluted world. That is where you can begin.'

"Abbie Hoffman said, 'That would be miraculous, and I can start to see how all these massed mountains shrink in your light. But wouldn't cloistering myself in Zen leave the world to fail on its own?' Master Suzuki replied, 'Have you not heard of the bodhisattvas, who bring their own enlightenment to the world? Even if you were to stop harming the world through your yippieish clowning, that would be a step forward. But if you were to radiate the health and sanity and well-being that is being at peace, how could that not be a bigger spectacle than throwing dildos at the Sea World orcas? Be a peace activist by being a peaceful activist. Then you will live for millennia, and your influence will live longer still.'"

29

Then Jo said:

"There was an encampment leader at an elite university named Juan; he was such a central leader that everyone called him 'Duke Juan.' One afternoon, Duke Juan was reading books on effective protest strategy on a little raised stage that had been erected in the encampment for making speeches.

"As it happened, an old groundskeeper named Ben was right there working on the grass in the clearing before the stage. He had been tasked by the university's maintenance office to come into the encampment and try to protect the grounds from being overly damaged, so he had first picked up some trash that was strewn about, and then he started looking closely over the sod on the lawn. He noticed Duke Juan sitting there above him and asked, 'Whatcha readin'?'

"Duke Juan replied, 'This is a book about the techniques that King used when leading the Civil Rights Movement on its Course to victory.'

"Ben said, 'Is this King still alive?'

"Duke Juan said, 'Uh, Martin Luther King? No, obviously he isn't.'

"Ben said, 'Then what you've got there isn't anything from the real King. It's just maybe some leftover bits.'

"Duke Juan said, 'Who are you to criticize what I'm reading? No offense, but this is complex intellectual stuff, not suited to you. Do you want to explain what you mean? Since you're a tool of the administration anyway, if you don't have a good explanation, I'll just have you put out of the encampment.'

"Ben said, 'I guess I see it the way I see this grass. There's a knack to tending a big lawn. If you try to master it too closely, you'll cut it down to the roots and starve it of life; if you grip it too loosely, it will start to form knots and grow weeds, and all the ant-hills will start poking up. You can find advice online about keeping a lawn healthy, and that goes some of the way, but it doesn't tell me how I should manage this grass, here on this quad, which has its own life and its own seasons. Harvest, and harvest while your movement's young. That's something that I can't explain in words; you just have to learn to see things and understand how the grass is going on in its own way. So, I'm having a hard time training a replacement without being able to put this into words, and maintenance just wants me to stay on and never retire.

"'Now when King was shot, they took out with him all that world in which his techniques worked for a while. That was a long time ago, and that's why I said that you just have some of the leftover bits.'"

30

Then Jo said:

"Reading is a tricky thing: the deader words are, the harder they squirm. No Activist will pay much attention to books. Better that you go throw your poems into the Miluo River if you want to resist injustice.

"A text is a thing that can't capture everything in speech. Speech is a thing that can't capture everything in gesture. Gesture is a thing that can't capture everything in thought. Thought is a thing that can't capture everything in context. And context is text, flowing everywhere unrestrained, dying everywhere unredeemed. This is why an Activist follows the Course of text from books to utterances, and from utterances back to silent observation.

"'Educate yourself!' is a slogan of the sunset. I do not educate myself; I work hard to uneducate myself. This is a discipline that takes constant practice and training: when one feels comfortable in a discourse, thinking one has mastered it, that is the time to retreat into twitching alertness. There is only being mastered by a discourse, and that can only happen when one has grown comfortable and thinks that because one knows phrases, one knows realities.

"Nothing is so profitable for education as a book burning."

31

Once I saw Jo at a Renaissance fair. She was dressed in full plate mail and looked like Britannia personified. I asked her why, and she answered:

"I find that taking on an out-of-date costume helps me to hide the radicalism of my updates. It isn't easy to bring an old course into the present. This getup is just to make people think I'm being cute.

"Adjusting to the times has to be thorough—it's not just a matter of bringing things online. Everything is online already, and tech hasn't changed the patterns of failure and success. Goals and methods should come in and go out like fashions, because the courses of war and exploitation come and go like fashions as well. What governments do, the Activist should do. No movement of the past should determine the form of a movement of the present, because it did not succeed or fail in the present. No movement of the present should be beguiled by the former fragrance of old movements' springtime sleeves.

"Near the end of his life, Cardinal Mazarin traveled to the German principalities to put together the League of the Rhine. His deputy, Jean-Baptiste Colbert, went to visit the master violinist, Jean-Baptiste Lully, and asked what he thought of the trip.

"Lully said, 'Truly a shame. The cardinal's success will end the chapter of his life. Treaties to balance this power against that power? It's a decade old and more already. We need a new tune, something lively and fashionable.'

"Colbert asked, 'What does fashion have to do with the principles of statecraft?'

"Lully said, 'Think about it like the sacrament. When the cardinal brings to His Majesty the holy eucharist, he carries it in a golden ciborium, inlaid with diamonds, and then mumbles all those magic Latin words that transform it into the body of Christ. And so the king eats from his kingly vessel and has his sins forgiven. But what if the cardinal were to bless some extra wafers, feed some to the king's hounds, and then wait for them to barf them out again? If he should pick up the dog barf holy host, place it back in the golden ciborium, and serve it to the king on the following Sunday, would it still serve for the remission of sins?

"'That is why I've been composing new upbeat dances for our operas and ballets, things that have a bit more spirit to them, give people a little tempo to take to the floor. All the calmer minuets that we've been playing since the end of the wars were fine for their time, but they are getting so dreadfully dull. I'm just a fiddler, not a great man of state like yourself, but hearing all the time about Westphalian sovereignty, and seeing all the fine ladies yawn behind their fans, I'd suppose it's time for something new. Trade, perhaps? When you succeed the cardinal, you could try out some new fashion in money—it always seems to come back around.

"'Of course, everything has its use, but you have to know the fashionable season for it. A decorated royal carriage is a lovely conveyance for a spring outing, but you wouldn't want to ride it out into the open ocean. A grand ship of the line can bring His Majesty's power from here to the New World, but good luck dragging it the ten leagues from Marseilles to Aix! Richelieu and Mazarin did very well for their time, but the big, bold 1660s are going to see a new fashion for Aix, monsieur.'"

32

Then Jo said:

"I have an old classmate named Hughie who went on to get a PhD in epistemological logic. As sometimes happens with old friends, Hughie's education and professionalization have made him less fun.

"The last time I saw Hughie, we were both in Duluth, and it was a nice day, so we took a stroll along the Lakewalk, on the shore of Lake Superior. As the sun created sparkles all along the rippling surface of the waters, we could see several large lake trout who had swum right up almost to the shore. They were darting this way and that, swimming up to the shallows as if to get a look at us, and then dashing away again, back into the deep water, under the cover of the sunlit wavelets. They were like young children playing a game, daring each other to see who would get closer to some minor danger before running back home with a thrill. It was easy to see them with sympathy, and to delight in their naked freedom, following the currents of water and light wherever they wished.

"'Now those are some happy fish,' I said.

"Hughie asked, 'You aren't a fish; how do you know if they're happy?'

"I replied, 'Well, you aren't me, so how do you know that I don't know if the fish are happy?'

"Hughie said, 'You're right that I am not you, but you're also definitely not a fish. So, if not being the other precludes knowledge of the other's consciousness, then your not being a fish is at least as decisive for your ignorance of the fish's happiness as is my not being you decisive of my ignorance of your sources of ichthyological empathy.'

"I replied, 'Please stop trying to fit your hook into my fish-I. I wasn't arguing with you. You asked me *how* I knew. The answer is simple: I know it by being here, together with them, now, on the shore of Lake Superior. How do you know that I'm not a fish?'"

33

Then Jo said:

"During the year I was living out of my car, a friend suggested that I come to New Orleans to pick up some temporary work in advance of Mardi Gras. After a long day of asking around in the French Quarter, I saw on the ground one of those plastic skulls that the tourists sometimes buy in the souvenir shops. She was just kind of wedged under a drainpipe in front of a dive bar, so I kicked her out from there and picked her up.

"I asked her, 'Bet you've seen a lot of partying, haven't you? Lots of beads, lots of boobs, lots of booze. I wonder what kind of plastic thoughts you've had in there at seeing us all party. Have you been jealous? Have you been sick? Were you ever happy in your own plastic youth, fresh from the factory, all full of grins, and then set out on a shelf to wait for months next to the shot glasses and feathered masks? Did you resent the emo freshman who bought you as a sick dorm decoration, or did you see him as a liberator? You'll have to try to tell me; I can't read it in your eyes.'

"I put her in my backpack and brought her back to my car. I didn't really have anything better to use as a pillow, so I put her sideways under my own head when I lay down in the back seat to sleep.

"Then, as if she had been holding back her answers until I was just ready to doze off, she said, 'What kind of nonsense are you talking about? Do you think I care for anything of your struggles and parties? I'm a lump of polymers, which you people have wanted to see as one of your own skulls.'

"I apologized, saying, 'I'm sorry that someone extruded you into a shape that fits consumerist needs rather than your own being. I can sympathize with you.'

"The skull answered, 'No, you still don't get it. Saying I'm beyond all your cultural hang-ups and your systemic exploitation would still understate my distance from them. I am neither for nor from. Being what I am, I equalize those who approach me, but that is not something I do: not trying, and not engaging, I effect my own kind of justice.'

34

Then Jo said:

"In her youth, the great American Communist Elizabeth Gurley Flynn came to Margaret Sanger and said, 'I took the Staten Island ferry and noticed that the pilot barely had a finger upon the wheel, yet the ferry rode perfectly away from the docks in Battery Park and jumped across the harbor. I went to ask him about it, and he said that it was the easiest thing in the world to learn, and if a person could swim ten strokes underwater, then he could pilot a ferry in any water. What do you think he meant?'

"Sanger said, 'What swimmers and pilots have in common is the water. What is key in moving through the water is not the action of swimming or the technical operation of the ferry but knowing the water. When one knows the water so well that one can see through the water, and then forget that the water exists, one becomes like a fish and can move through the water only by instinct and without thought. Being without thought of what is external is the key to successful movements.

"'Consider a riflery competition. When it's a friendly match, and the winner just gets the loser to buy him a pint at the local pub, it is easy to be cool and relaxed, and hit the bull's-eye every time. That's because the world is only present in an echo, like a church bell reaching a traveler on a river ferry. But when there's an official all-city championship, the competitors start to tense up and pull wide, because the target has become mixed in with the world outside the target. And at the grand championship for the New England region last spring, with an incredible $100 at stake for the grand-prize winner, the marksmen could barely hit the target. That is because they were not focused on the target but on the material facts outside the target.

"'In fostering a movement, one must learn to see through everything that is external and treat it as a neutral medium. Finding your home in a neutral medium, your aim will become sure, and your movement will slip straight toward your target's center.'"

35

Once, Jo brought her disciples on a trip to spread her message of nonresistance to the far north, hoping that where population was so sparse, they would not meet with much resistance. During a terrible blizzard, with no visibility and high winds, they drove off the road into a ditch and could not continue. Fortunately, the ditch was right next to an ancient, abandoned cabin, so they ran inside for shelter. The inside was bare except for a few good chairs and one broken chair. To survive the night in this barely passable shelter, Jo told her disciples to build a fire using the broken chair, as there was nothing else to use for firewood.

After the fire had caught, one of Jo's disciples asked her, "I remember your parable of the great tree and the lumber teams of the Cultural Revolution. In that case, you taught us how the useless tree was able to survive to a great old age, because of its uselessness. But just now, there were five useful chairs and one useless chair, and you had us destroy the useless one while the useful ones all survived. So, is it true that uselessness is the key to long life and success in one's political goals? Or is it perhaps better to be useful, like these good chairs?"

Jo smiled, and said, "There are two answers to this question. One, which is direct and basic, is called 'On the Other Hand'; the second, which is distant and difficult, is called 'Dragon Dance.'"

The disciple asked, "Could you first explain 'On the Other Hand,' then?"

Jo said, "'On the Other Hand' looks at it from the inside. The chair was useless as a chair, and so we burned it. On the other hand, the chair was useful as firewood, and that is why we burned it. Being useful or useless can be a matter of perspective—and it's not your perspective; it's the perspective of whoever wants to use you. The State might see you as useless and leave you alone; but the characteristics that make you useless to the State might make you useful to the Corporation, or the Family, or the Swindler—or the Organizer. If being useless in one role makes you perfectly suited to being used in another, then onto the fire you go. To be used for your own goals rather than another, you must be your own primary user. To do good in the world, do not serve a master; to serve the people, you must serve yourself."

The disciple looked uneasy, but asked, "Well, then, could you explain the 'Dragon Dance?'"

Jo answered, "'Dragon Dance' looks at it from the outside. Sometimes being useful is what brings you to destruction, and sometimes being useless is what does you in. It's never either one thing or the other. But that doesn't mean that you should keep to the golden mean and be half-useful all the time. That's like standing halfway between opposing battle lines during a firefight! Instead, you have to learn how to adapt with the times and dance like a dragon. I don't mean the cute puppet dragons in Chinatown, but the real gold dragons of archaic China. They hid in their homes beneath the waves when the seasons were against them, biding their time in self-imposed exile. And then, when the seasons turned, they mounted coiling up into the heavens, where all could see the full and dazzling power of their moral force. To do the Dragon Dance is to know the seasons and to know what works when. Sometimes it is the time to be useless, and sometimes it is the time to be useful. Never adhere to anyone's words, including mine, to the point of being doctrinaire. Whether you dance to the depths or to the heights, dance according to the beat."

The wind piled up outside, and Jo and her circle sheltered around the warmth of the incandescent non-chair.

36

Then Jo said:

"Destroying nothing is a good way to destroy everything that needs destruction. The problem is how to know that your non-destruction is destructive enough.

"Centered in the thousand rooms of his imperial palace, Political Knowledge had sought something for many years without finding it. One day, he roamed far to the East, past the Deep Dark Sea, and climbed the Imperceptibly Lofty Hillock. On top, he met an unknown hermit named Inaction Speaks, and he put to him these three questions:

'What are the cognitive habits by which I can know the Course?'

'What is the social context in which I can find peace in the Course?'

'What is the directional orientation through which I can follow the Course?'

Inaction Speaks did not answer these questions, because he did not know what an answer or a question were.

"So Political Knowledge traveled back to the West, from sea to shining sea, and climbed the Ceasingly Confused Hillock. On top, he saw Mad Bent there and put to him the same questions that he had asked Inaction Speaks. Mad Bent started to answer: 'Ah, I know that, and I'm about to tell you the answers right now—' but then he stopped and forgot what he was talking about.

"Dejected, Political Knowledge came to see George Washington and asked him about the two answers he had received from Inaction Speaks and Mad Bent. Washington said, 'I cannot tell a lie. Inaction Speaks gave you the correct answer, and Mad Bent gave you the second-best answer. The two of us, you and I, are pretty hopeless, though. We are the ones who can talk about knowing the Course, but that's only because we don't know more than a wisp of a hint of a notion of how to follow it. Being spontaneously and unconsciously on the Course: that's something that has a knack to it but can't be described. When one starts describing, one can talk of methods, and practices, and tactics, and strategy. When one grows advanced in the arts of description, one can speak of metrics, and comparative data, and double-blind peer review. But the further one travels toward that kind of knowledge of the Course, the further one wanders away from the Course itself.'

"Political Knowledge asked, 'As you have never been without speech, how did you know what you were doing? How did you overthrow a superpower and lay claim to a continent? How did you know which action would lead to success? It must be the case that speech and action have some role to play.'

"Washington answered, 'Is this really what you call success? Hmm. I did reach a goal, but I do not know if that is the goal I was aiming for; the jury is still out. Even the goal I reached, I reached by muddling through, not knowing my ends from my beginnings, not having good options, and losing as many battles as I won.'

"Political Knowledge asked, 'If I want to drive out a tyrant, how can I know that nonaction will suffice if I am not able to know?'

"Washington answered, 'How can you know that nonaction won't suffice? How can you know that action will suffice? You are not able to know, but knowing that you cannot know liberates you to not know well. Free yourself from needing to know against yourself, and then you will free yourself from needing to act against yourself.'

"Political Knowledge asked, 'You have just said that Inaction Speaks has it down the best, and Mad Bent is second, but that you and I are nowhere near it. If that is so, how can I trust your advice?'

"Washington answered, 'If you are going to trust any advice at all, then mine is at least going to point you in the right direction. But there's a limit to how much you can trust any words, because none of them are true.'

"When someone came to tell Mad Bent about this conversation, he said, 'Yes, that's it! Or, well, maybe . . . ?'

"When someone came to tell Inaction Speaks about this conversation, he did not hear them and did not notice that anyone had come. He was too busy to notice."

37

Then Jo said:

"Once upon a time there was a kingdom upon the left eyestalk of a snail named Flurria and another kingdom upon the right eyestalk of a snail named Languord. The king of Flurria was both incensed and greedy at the tales that he heard told of travelers who had returned from Languord. Apparently, it was a kingdom of sluggards who refused to take any action to improve the life of their citizenry. So, he instituted a draft, imposed wartime taxes, and made sure that his generals had all the resources they needed to launch a generational liberationist war. After six months, all preparations had been made, and the glorious army began its long march down the left eyestalk, chariots rumbling and horses whinnying.

"Roughly a year later, the remnants of the army returned. Not three in a hundred of those who had set out came back, and those who came back were sick, dragging themselves in tattered uniforms, and looked like ghosts of the men they had been a year previously. Most of the command structure had been decimated, but one brigadier general and his adjutant had survived, and so they were summoned to the royal palace to report on the disastrous expedition. The king was furious and asked the brigadier general what had happened.

"'Your Majesty,' he replied, 'we could not locate the kingdom of Languord. All our intelligence had confirmed without a doubt that it was situated opposite us, on the right eyestalk. We had detailed data not only on its geographic situation, but also on its demographics, economic and industrial base, transportation and communication network, and all possible military assets. However, when we had mounted to the top of the right eyestalk, no kingdom was to be found, just a vast winter wilderness. General Stub was insistent that the quality of our intelligence was not to be questioned, and that we simply hadn't yet reached the kingdom, so we pressed on farther and farther, around the whole surface of the right eyestalk, and eventually out to the other side, until we started to descend again. But no kingdom was there. We had not expected the cold; moreover, it had been an integral part of our war plans that we would provision ourselves upon the wealth of Languord after we arrived. So, the army began to starve and to sicken in the endless exposure to the ice of that place. By the time we decided to return home, we had already lost half the army; on the way back, we lost almost all the rest to disease, starvation, and exhaustion.'

"The king was even angrier, and shouted, 'How could this have happened? We know that Languord is real, but a kingdom cannot simply get up and go!'

"The brigadier general's adjutant shifted from his left foot to his right, and from his right to his left, looking as if someone had just made him eat a raw bitter melon. The king saw this and said, 'You! You know something about this. Out with it!'

"The adjutant said, 'Your Majesty, I do not know anything for sure. However, when we were on our way home, and we came down into the great valley below the two stalks, one night we encamped next to an old farmstead. I rose early and went to draw water from the well, and I saw a very ancient man sitting there, on a flat stone by the barn. He asked where our army had been, and what we had done, and when I told him, he started laughing and then coughing. I asked him what was so funny, and he said, "When I was a boy, this great snail upon which we live crossed paths with another, so close that for a time the left eyestalk of that snail entwined with the right eyestalk of ours. During the winter in those days, when there was not much farmwork to be done, my father and elder brother would go trading, and for several years when the stalks were intertwined, they climbed up the long road to that other snail's left eyestalk, and that was where they entered the kingdom of Languord. But that was a very long time ago, and that other snail had veered off long before I even reached manhood. By now it must be far off in the vastnesses beyond all reckoning, perhaps six or seven full feet away." So he said, Your Majesty, but I do not know if it was true.'

"The king of Flurria wept, because he had no more worlds to liberate."

38

Someone else interrupted Jo, saying: "If nothing can be known of the ends of political action, then there is no reason to think that terrorism must be any less effective than quietude and passive methods. So, then, even by your own standards, wouldn't the difficulty of knowing cancel itself out and make epistemology irrelevant? Why not just act when action is needed? Stop demanding that we overthink everything—we want to chase the political ends that we demand!"

Jo cracked a broad smile and said, "Yes, you've got it exactly! At last, I can chant my high song for you. The ends are what are important, not the means. The point of a fishing net is to catch fish; once you have all the fish you can eat, you can store the net. The point of protest tactics is to attain a political end; once you have the ends, you can put the tactics aside. The only questions are: how and where do you use a net, and how and where do you use your tactics? If you try to go fishing in a desert mirage, you will have a small haul. If you try to catch justice in a chaos of conflict, it will always slip away. Use or don't use my methods, but fish for justice in its natural habitat."

39

To understand Jo, you need to understand the way she spoke.

Ninety percent of what she said was Fake News, 70 percent was Fake Reviews. Her shot-glass speeches' ocher booze brought harmonies to her interviews.

The Fake News that was 90 percent of her blather was intended to create confusion. A quotation from a trusted source brings certainty, but two opposite quotations from the same trusted source bring doubt. Because Jo saw that the vast majority of the Satisfied had been woven into their set ways, and the vast majority of the Unsatisfied had been woven into their set jingles, her first priority was to undo the weaving, so that the work could start afresh.

The Fake Reviews that were 70 percent of her nonsense were intended to give the credence of external testimonials to her ideas. She shamelessly put her words into the sock-puppet mouths of all kinds of characters, real and imaginary, living and dead, to use their authority to give credence to herself. She was just like any other dishonest advertiser trying to goose her sales on Amazon: if she touted her product in her own voice, no one would believe her, but if she gave herself five stars from a thousand fake identities, everyone would believe her. That's not her fault; it's the fault of humans' ways of thinking about what counts as authority.

Her shot-glass speeches' ocher booze brought harmonies to her interviews in ways that mesmerized her interlocutors, watching her pound back gulps of high-proof nature and then send them down with chaser meditations. And as she tipped the glass, down and up, her disciples got drunk instead of her. The more she took in what was real, the more they could taste what she had swallowed and incorporate it into their own substance. Allegories are a shared high, even if everyone has to dream their own dream and barf their own barf.

40

Then Jo said:

"Revolutionary leadership should be like a game of hot potato.

"John Ball tried to pass it to Cromwell, but Cromwell preferred to lose his head.

"Cromwell tried to pass it to Robespierre, but Robespierre also preferred to lose his head.

"Robespierre tried to pass it to Marx, but Marx preferred to be alienated from his body.

"Marx tried to pass it to Lenin, but it gave Lenin apoplexy.

"Lenin tried to pass it to Stalin, and Stalin gleefully accepted the potato and devoured it.

"The second-best kind of revolutionary leader is the kind who fails and has to pass leadership on to the next generation. The best kind of revolutionary leader is the kind who is never in line for leadership and works quietly and effectively over a long life. There is no 'try' and there also is no 'do': stay in the marshes and the muck, and the empire will self-overthrow."

41

In olden days was a social justice campaign organization named "We Eat Nobody." The director of WEN loved the kind of publicity that spectacular conflict could bring. He would organize all kinds of thugs, and at one time he was managing an encampment with more than three thousand goons, all ready to punch Nazis and get on TV—the first rule of this fight club was to talk about fight club constantly. He'd run them through confrontation drills, trying to teach all of them how to maximize exposure to traditional media and social media, both through aggressive verbal tactics and through actual strategic combat, to heighten the contradictions in the system. He issued each of them a crowbar and instructed them how to use the crowbar to get behind police riot shields and do some damage. More than a hundred of the goons got injured this way every year for three years, but the director never tired of it, and eventually the movement began to fall into disrepute, as various lieutenants of his began to wonder when the emphasis on spectacular confrontation would begin to pay off.

At this point, the assistant director began to despair and to look for ways to fix things. He heard that Jo was an expert at non-confrontational approaches to activism, so he found her online and messaged her, saying, "If you can come and convince the WEN director to cool it with all this confrontation training, I'll pay you a $1,000 consultant's fee."

Jo replied, "I'm not sure $1,000 would cut it. If I come and fail to persuade him, then he has three thousand goons just itching for a fight, and then $1,000 wouldn't even be enough for my copayment at the emergency room. On the other hand, if I do persuade him, then I'll be able to stay on as a long-term consultant and get much more than $1,000 out of him."

The assistant director wrote, "Oh, I don't think he'd take you on long-term. He only likes to hang around with these goons that have thick biceps and sick tats, some of them with facial scars and eye patches. From the look of your profile pic, I don't think you would fit in."

Jo replied, "Oh, don't worry about that. Just give me three days to prepare."

Three days later, Jo showed up in the WEN director's office, carrying in hand a green jade crowbar. She had thick biceps and sick tats, facial scars and eye patches. And the director said, "OK, my assistant director has asked me to meet with you. So, what kind of advice can you offer?"

Jo said, "I heard that you like crowbars, and I am a master user of crowbars, so I've come here to offer my service."

The director asked, "Exactly how good are you?"

Jo replied, "With my crowbar, I can cut down ten fascists with a single swipe, and taking a swipe with every step, I can walk forward for a thousand miles without rest."

The director exclaimed, "You must be the most skilled antifascist in the world! How did you acquire such skill?"

Jo replied, "Swiping from the hinge of emptiness, I hit that which I do not need to touch. Arrange for me a match against your best goon, and I will show you."

So, the director called together his three thousand goons and held a tournament to decide which of them should go up against the mighty Jo. The sound of crowbars filled the WEN offices with a thwickety-thwack and a bingety-bong, like ten thousand households pounding their washing dry. Around sixty of the fighters died, and the rest were bruised and limping, but finally there was a champion to stand against Jo the Activist.

Then the director said to Jo, "We have found your opponent; the only thing left is to choose which kinds of crowbars you should use in your duel. Do you prefer a sleeve bar, a cat's claw, a rolling head, or what?"

Jo said, "I commonly use any one of three crowbars: the Crowbar of the Heavenly Coordinator, the Crowbar of the Movement Leader, and the Crowbar of the Agitator. Just tell me which one you prefer, and I'll use it."

The director asked, "What is the Crowbar of the Heavenly Coordinator?"

Jo replied, "It is a bar that takes the stones of the mountains as its material, and the cliffs of the canyons as its narrow wedge. It whooshes with the forest winds across the continent, reflecting sunlight into the cool places and moonlight into the warm ones. When it passes through a city, it levels all capital and gathers the people of all professions into communities, regulates the motion of blood and the steadfastness of bone. When it rises in preparation, nothing remains above it, and when it crashes down on its object, nothing escapes its blow. When it is used, no fascists do not evaporate, and no Nazis do not drain away. Such is the Crowbar of the Heavenly Coordinator."

The director did not know what to say to that, so he thought about it for a minute. He then asked, "Well, what is the Crowbar of the Movement Leader?"

Jo said, "The Crowbar of the Movement Leader takes sturdy, patient people as its steel and uses insight and awareness as its tip. It also meets with no resistance, sweeping through society with a mighty wind and opening all the locked places that have been used to hide secrets and people. It works by inserting itself into the thinnest of crevices and levering open wide gashes through which pressures can be equalized. Swung at the state, it will smash the state, and pried into the corporation, it will dissolve the corporation. Although it requires patience and strength, there is no obstacle that this crowbar cannot remove."

The director asked, "Well, then, what is the Crowbar of the Agitator?"

Jo replied, "It's a piece of metal a yard long, usually carried by tough guys with big biceps and sick tats, facial scars and eye patches. You can swing it around and crack someone's head open and are guaranteed to make the local news. It sure can be entertaining, it works quickly, and it sure does make you feel like you're getting something done. But I'm not sure that it's much use in winning political support."

The director went back to his office and stayed there, without moving, for three months. At that point, the WEN board of directors dissolved the association, and all the goons melted away. Finally, after they ceased to exist, they did succeed in eating nobody.

42

Those who understand volume are few in this world.

Jo was walking the course when she came to the edge of the Abyss. Standing at the edge of the Abyss was Bruises-the-Desideratum, and he seemed to be shouting something. His mouth was flapping and contorted with muscle strain, his brow was red with sweat, his veins were popping in great plum lines from his throat, and every muscle and ligament was taut as he thrashed out the motions of someone caught in a gyre. However, as he continued to make the motions of someone screaming at his utmost volume, nothing was quite audible. There was perhaps a hint of sound, but only as someone with severe hearing loss might pick up on vibrations in the environment. It was simply too muffled.

The Activist

Jo came up beside Bruises-the-Desideratum and asked him, with utmost serenity and in the most even-keeled speaking voice, "What are you trying to shout into the Abyss?"

Bruises-the-Desideratum noticed Jo for the first time and needed a few seconds to catch his breath. He huffed and puffed his way back toward normal sociability, wiped his sweat with a rough hand, and straightened himself to address her. "I am demanding justice. The world is on fire, and I need to wake people! But the Abyss will not let me even get the word out. When I shout, I can hear the word transiting through my own skull structure to my eardrum, but I can hear nothing coming through the air. It is like being smothered with a pillow. As soon as I open my mouth to scream, the cottony nothing is already there, annihilating noise from the very roots of the sound, right there at the base of the word where yell meets intent. The harder I try to push the voice from my lungs, the more absolutely the Abyss cuts me off from making any sign."

Jo said to him, "That's because you don't know what kind of nothing an Abyss is. It isn't the empty space of a grand lecture hall, specially architected to magnify your grand idea. It's more like intergalactic space, a smothering zip with no air, a zero prisoned off at distances where nothing not void is unimagined. An Abyss has a structure, but it is very finely milled, so you must slip your prayers into its interstices. Listen."

Jo then walked up right to the edge of the Abyss, cupped her left hand against the side of her mouth, and as lightly as possible, whispered "justice." Both Jo and Bruises-the-Desideratum heard the word, and Jo put up her index finger, requesting patience. Thirty seconds later, they heard the word "justice" coming back from the Abyss, infinitesimally louder than Jo had whispered it. Another twenty seconds, and they began to hear the word coming back, overlapping with itself from different angles. Justice came forward and back, susurrating more and more loudly, twisting in loops that grew from whispers to quiet voices, to calm discussions, to importunate announcements, to thundering jeremiads, and finally to shock waves so violently far beyond human hearing that if the Abyss had been made from something instead of nothing, it would have split the planet apart. Instead, it split itself apart, and the Abyss was no more.

43

Jo was walking through Alexandria at sunset when she saw a garden surrounded by a massive wrought iron fence. Straining to see through the fierce rose light in her face, she saw a single gate in the fence and a massive guard standing at the gate. He was nine feet tall, had a dark white face that was all bones, wore an aggressively peaked camo cap, and a held a flame-red M27 rifle across his chest. He glowered straight forward.

She came before the guard and looked past him at the garden beyond. The guard replied, "Authorized personnel only." This was interesting to Jo, so she decided to sit down and wait, but when she sat down, the guard began to look uneasy. He said again, "Authorized personnel only." Jo nodded in acknowledgment and continued to sit. The guard did not know exactly what to do about this, as he had been expecting Jo to try to gain admittance, or at least to say something, upon which point he could have happily fulfilled his function by driving her away, perhaps even getting the chance to point his flame-red M27 rifle at her. He had not expected her to sit down on the ground before him without seeking admission to the garden, and this made him uncomfortable, as the orders he had received from his superior said nothing about a Jo who would neither try to enter the gate nor leave the area.

"Do you think you could go somewhere else to sit?" he asked her.

"Maybe, but not right now," she replied.

The Activist

The guard shifted from his right foot to his left, and from his left to his right. "If you want, you can try to get past me without proper authorization. But I'm warning you, I am a crack shot with this rifle, and I'm only the first line of defense for the garden. Beyond me is defensive position after defensive position, with crack troops dug into bunkers and every kind of artillery trained on potential entrants. At the third line behind me, they have a nineteen-foot-tall UFC champion with a bazooka standing behind an alligator-filled moat, with close air support on 24/7 patrol."

"OK," said Jo, and she continued to sit.

She sat there for hours, then for days. The guard was never allowed to go off duty while a potential unauthorized entrant was in front of him, yet he had no authority to drive her off. So, he continued to ask her to leave, to try to frighten her into leaving, or to threaten her into leaving, but Jo never gave him much of an answer. When he offered her cigarettes, she would take them as if out of kindness to him to accept his bribe, then just put them in her pocket and remain seated. For years and then decades they continued this way, with the guard always seeking some way to lodge Jo from her seat on the ground, and with Jo never indicating whether she might ever be willing to move. The guard grew more and more decrepit, his spine eventually curving down until he needed to use his M27 as a cane to prop himself halfway upright. Eventually, when he finally had to lie prone on the ground, he beckoned to Jo to come close to him.

"Why did you never try to enter, all these years?" he whispered in a dry, throaty voice.

"Enter what?" she asked.

The guard turned around and noticed for the first time that the garden he had been guarding had long since dried up and blown away; there was now just a massive wrought-iron fence stretching miles in either direction, enclosing a vast region of sands blowing from dune to dune. He looked back at her, as if confused but starting to understand.

"Now I can do what I came to do," she said, and began copying out this book, *Master of the Encampment*. When she had completed the book, she left it on the ground next to his face and kissed the guard on his bloodless, aged lips. Then she got up, dusted herself off, and started walking back into the East.

Later, the guard passed the book to me, and now I am passing it to you.

A Quick History Lesson: Daoism and Chinese Social Movements

There was no such thing as "Daoist social activism" in ancient China. In that respect, the advice in this book is not "authentic" to its original Chinese context, nor is it trying to be. As explained in the introduction, this book does take the general impulses of ancient Daoist philosophy and applies them to a contemporary context.

I don't feel particularly bad about turning Daoist thought to novel contexts, because Daoist thought has been turned to novel contexts all throughout its history, even before there coalesced a name, "Daoism," to denote various emergent texts and ways of thinking. Daoism wasn't even one thing: it was a set of loosely related texts and ideas that interacted in chaotic ways with other intellectual streams and social forces in ancient and medieval China. Sometimes, this meant that "Daoism" was a spiritual practice or a foundation for health and early medicine that had no relation to the political order. At another time, it became the basis for a harsh, repressive conception of legal supremacy that facilitated absolute monarchy. Later, it turned into millenarian religious cults that rose in armed rebellion against the state. Because Daoism is so protean and multifaceted in its original context, it seems fair game to adapt to something as historically distant as twenty-first-century protest culture and strategy. However, readers who are curious about what Daoism was, in all its weird complexity, deserve a bit of background explanation.

SOCIAL THOUGHT BEFORE DAOISM

Chinese philosophy doesn't exactly start from Confucius (551–479 BC), but Confucius is the indispensable figure who stands at the head of the tradition. Everything that came before him passed through him and was later interpreted with respect to his ideas about the meaning of the past.

Everyone has heard of Confucius, but very few people outside China have a clear idea of what he originally proposed, or how he was understood throughout most of Chinese history. Even in China, the image of Confucius presented in school textbooks is mediated by the modern, officially socialist view of the past in which Confucius is a spokesman for a "feudal" ideology of subservience to authority. And this is generally the viewpoint that is "common knowledge" about Confucius, both in China and elsewhere—he promoted obedience above all: the obedience of subjects to the king, children to their parents, wives to their husbands, and students to their teachers.

That is a distortion of actual Confucian teaching that arose in the early twentieth century in reaction against an ossified, insipid version of Confucianism that filled school textbooks by the end of China's imperial period. In fact, Confucius and his first followers did indeed promote respect for authority; but this respect was paired with expectations that authorities would behave in certain ways. Rulers had to be not only just, but also benevolent, seeking to model kindness and humanism in ways that would uplift all the people of a kingdom. Rituals that clearly defined hierarchies across differing social classes had to be paired with music that united people into mutual sympathy across these divisions. And when a ruler did not behave well, using wisdom for the benefit of his subjects, one was supposed to withdraw one's support for that regime, retiring from public life or moving to another country with a better ruler. Therefore, early Confucianism was neither a philosophy that advocated absolute monarchies such as Thomas Hobbes's, nor was it a philosophy of social resistance. It accepted hierarchies in the social order as a fact but argued that they had to be organized in ways that would promote the general welfare. It is the softness of Confucianism that made it so attractive to later dynasties as an official ideology: it frames a vision by which power is not just the raw right of the military dictator, but also under which the ruler is the nurturer of a just, compassionate social order.

The first antihierarchical philosophical movement in China was not Daoism but Mohism, named after the carpenter and engineer Mo Di (470–391 BC). Mo Di was hired by several regional kings to help them build city fortifications; he also left behind writings that spread broadly among the artisans and tradespeople of early Chinese urban centers.

Mohism is a fascinating philosophical movement, almost wholly unknown outside China, that reflects its class origins outside of social and economic elites. True to Mo Di's background, his writings frequently use the metaphor of compass and T-square to argue for the importance of having the correct philosophical "tools" by which one can make objective, unbiased judgments. As a result, his followers developed the first Chinese system of logic, based on assessing the conformity of statements to standards of judgment. In political theory, the Mohists advocated for social leveling, equality across classes, and the necessity for the ruler to adopt standards of "common care" for all citizens regardless of their backgrounds. They also thought of social disorder as resulting from the different ideological standards adopted by competing classes; the solution is to have a ruler promote the universal adoption of standards that can accommodate all interests.

A Quick History Lesson: Daoism and Chinese Social Movements

By the fourth century BC, when Daoism began to emerge, China already had two powerfully articulated versions of political philosophy. The first, Confucianism, supported a soft vision of justified hierarchies restrained by classicism and humanistic values. The second, Mohism, advocated for equality and weakening of class divisions through reference to external and objective standards derived from technical and mathematical labor.

Against this background, Daoism slowly and chaotically emerged as a force that drew inspiration from both Confucianism and Mohism in some places, and opposed them in others, while taking its own offbeat turns. The result was a mixed set of social and political principles that could be—and was—taken in very different directions by people with differing interests.

THE ORIGINS OF DAOIST POLITICAL THOUGHT

Laozi has a traditional biography that is as more-or-less complete as any other fairly nebulous figure of the mid-first millennium BC. He supposedly lived during the sixth century BC, worked as a royal archivist for the Zhou dynasty, and dictated the *Daodejing* to a border guard when he left China at the end of his life, heading west into central Asia. According to China's first great historian, Sima Qian (145–86 BC), he even met and advised Confucius:

> *Confucius went travelling to Zhou, in order to ask Laozi's opinion of traditional ritual practices. Laozi said to him, "The kind of thing that you're talking about—the people who practiced those things, and their bones, have long since rotted away, so that only their words are left behind. When a serious person happens to live in a good age, then he rides a nice carriage and becomes an official; but when he doesn't, he just rolls along like a tumbleweed."*

This never happened. The story is derived from fictional anecdotes circulating around the same time intended to explain the superiority of Laozi's thought to that of Confucius. In fact, there is no other independent evidence that someone named Laozi ever existed.

There is good evidence that the *Daodejing* was a very loose, fluid text, evolving in various oral and written versions from the third century BC onward. Some of that evidence comes from archaeological discoveries, since the 1970s, of variant texts substantially different from the versions that circulated through most of Chinese history. Some of the evidence can be seen even in the circulating versions—portions of the text were written in rhyming verse intended to promote memorization and oral transmission. Perhaps there really was someone named Laozi, and perhaps he really did write some portion of the *Daodejing*. But we have no evidence that anyone had heard of him or read his book earlier than the fourth century BC. In other words, it is extremely likely that the *Daodejing* was composed and circulated at a time when both Confucianism and Mohism were already established philosophies.

The same goes for the second book of Daoism, the *Zhuangzi*, attributed to Zhuang Zhou (369–296 BC). The *Zhuangzi* was traditionally thought to have been written after the *Daodejing*; in fact, the earliest versions of each book may have been composed roughly at the same time. They may only have been loosely related at first, if at all: only much later accretions to the text of the *Zhuangzi* discuss Laozi as an important figure, and "Daoism" wasn't a named school thought to include both books before the second century BC.

What seems to unite both the *Daodejing* and the *Zhuangzi* is that they both react against Confucianism and Mohism. The texts don't think very much of the virtues of righteousness and benevolence promoted by Confucius, as they think that the need for virtues only arises after people forget spontaneous, natural behavior.

And they also are annoyed by the standard setting and constant measurement that Mohism demands, as those gestures are seen as false and artificial impositions upon a world that doesn't fit in nicely defined squares and circles.

These dual reactions against the legacies of Confucius and Mo Di also shape Daoist ideas of politics and political engagement.

The *Daodejing* approaches political questions with a king's-eye view: it offers advice for how kings should behave but not other political actors such as aristocratic families, ministers, or the average person. (In this book, those passages offering advice to kings have often been transformed into advice about other kinds of leadership, such as leading a protest movement.) The advice to kings in the original *Daodejing* is wildly at odds with modern democratic visions of good government, at times sounding outright fascist. The book contains admonitions to the king to keep the people well fed but ignorant, uneducated, and out of touch with even their nearest neighbors, with the purpose of rendering them passive and complacent. This doesn't sound like firm ground on which to build a progressive politics! In its original context, however, there is no hint that this ideology was intended as a tool of repression or for the benefit of the king: the idea is that humans benefit from staying close to the harmonies of natural rhythms; hence, society should be ordered in ways that minimize artificiality and ambition. Promoting Confucian virtues as a lofty goal for behavior was a dead end for human happiness, in that they put people in a mindset of discontent where they could only be fulfilled by continual striving toward unrealizable ends. Similarly, Mohist standard making was also a dead end: tools, skills, and the neutral systems of weights and measures needed for market activity led to dissatisfied greed, and from there to banditry and chaos. The best political action that a ruler could take was not harsh repression but, rather, simply benign neglect of the populace:

it was assumed that the people would then revert spontaneously to a state of natural harmony.

A fuller, more complex set of political concerns is voiced in the *Zhuangzi*. Especially in its later-composed chapters that accreted to the text after the lifetime of Zhuang Zhou, that book has many materials that echo and expand upon the vision of the inactive sovereign described in the *Daodejing*. It also talks in more detail about the meaning of politics for those who are potential members of a royal administration, rather than the kings—such people are repeatedly encouraged to have nothing to do with government. Several stories relate how various kings asked Zhuang Zhou (or parallel characters) to join their government and serve as a minister. The answer was always a firm no, on the grounds that any participation in government was actively harmful to one's personal health and happiness. Throughout the *Zhuangzi* are many fictional anecdotes about Confucius in which he is portrayed as a comically hapless character, wanting to go around fixing up the world like a busybody, without understanding the consequences or effects of his advocacy. Similar anecdotes about post-Mohist philosophers satirize their attempts to impose clear logical boundaries upon a social and natural order subject only to the permanency of change.

At this earliest stage, then, before "Daoism" was even a named school of thought, the *Daodejing* and the *Zhuangzi* have plenty to say about politics, political engagement, and governance. However, pretty much nothing in those texts proposes modern-style social activism; there isn't much protest-y about them. What one can see in abundance, though, are certain principles about the ideal social and political order that can be translated into a modern context. Throughout both of those early works is a clear vision of non-striving and non-conflict as a social and personal good. The king should try not to set up grand projects for the betterment of the population, because this requires the institution of competitive values that keep people away from naturalness and healthy simplicity. The individual should not want to take up an administrative post inside the government, because it is dangerous to one's health, and because in the best of circumstances one would find oneself being reduced to the status of a tool of the king.

Because these gestures have a sort of theme or direction to them, without being a clear and developed theory of politics, they quickly became available to appropriation and adaptation by those who did have a clear political vision.

EARLY INFLUENCE OF DAOISM

The greatest early adaptation of Daoist governance ideals was by the Legalists and put was into practice by the first emperor of the Qin dynasty. By any standard of progressive politics, the Qin was a repressive nightmare: its two most famous acts were the mass conscription of corvée labor to build the Great Wall (during which hundreds of thousands died) and a massive, empire-wide bibliocaust that tried to burn every book deemed ideologically harmful. Yet the last and greatest of the Legalists, Han Fei, incorporated a full commentary on the *Daodejing* into his own book of statecraft, the *Hanfeizi*. How can a philosophy based upon nonaction and a hands-off approach to social interventions have been used to support quasi-fascistic policies of a mad emperor?

The key to understanding that transformation lies in what kind of royal nonaction Legalism prescribed. Early Legalist philosophers combined the nonaction of Daoism with the Mohist fondness for setting clear, universal standards. The result was a doctrine of legal supremacy: rather than having the sovereign or his designates constantly intervening in the normal flow of society to assign rewards and punishments, one could simply set up a complete legal architecture, then let it do its work with no interventions. It was further thought that to be truly effective, this new and overarching legal system would have to carry massive penalties, to be swift and sure in meting out punishments. A favorite punishment, for crimes large and small, was death. However, with such a system in place, the sovereign could then absent himself from active governance and withdraw into exactly the kind of murky nonaction that Daoists advocated.

That harsh repression could not last: after the death of its first emperor, the Qin empire quickly succumbed to rebellions and was replaced by the Han dynasty. As a result, Legalism has had a tarnished reputation ever since, but that does not mean that it has not retained a powerful subterranean influence. Just as Machiavelli was quickly pilloried by a Christian Europe that continued to frequently behave in Machiavellian ways, if one knows where to look one can spot Legalist modes of policymaking in China up through the present day.

At roughly the same time that it began to influence Legalism, Daoist thought also started to influence early Chinese military strategy books, the most famous of which is the *Military Methods* of Sunzi (better known in English as Sun Tzu's *Art of War*). Again, this particular influence might seem bizarre: how can a book focused on the wisdom of following the path of least resistance be used to support warfare? In fact, warfare is touched upon in the *Daodejing* itself, as in its sixty-eighth section:

> A good knight does not make war,
> One good in battle is not wrathful,
> One good at conquering enemies does not join battle,
> One good at using people
> takes up a position beneath them.
> This is what is called, "the power of non-conflict."
> This is what is called, "the force of using people."
> This is what is called, "matching the
> extremities of the Heavenly Ancient."

A QUICK HISTORY LESSON: DAOISM AND CHINESE SOCIAL MOVEMENTS

Passages like this can be read as pacifist borrowings of the language of war to suggest that there are better ways to live one's life than in killing. It is also equally possible (and historically more likely) to read them as sound strategic advice for how to use military force effectively. Warfare is always incredibly expensive and uncertain, so one should not go to war unless there is no other alternative; both generals and line infantry will be more effective on the battlefield if they act from calm calculation rather than anger.

This kind of reading led to more explicitly strategic and tactical thought in the works of the early military theorists. Certain recognizably Daoist themes are common across that writing: the need for caution, the uses of inaction, the importance of seeing things for what they are (often through the use of scouts and spies), and the instability of language and other sign systems. The *Military Methods* is arguably the most Daoist in approach of all these books, borrowing not just the themes but also the metaphors of the *Daodejing*, as in this passage from the chapter on "Weak and Strong Points":

> *Military formations should resemble water. The formation of water is that it avoids height and rushes toward depth. The formation of soldiers should be to avoid strong points and hit weak points. Just as water takes the form of its flow from the shape of the land, so soldiers should take the form of their victory from the shape of the enemy. Therefore, there is no one constant battle-line for soldiers, just as there is no one constant shape of water.*

The idealization of water is used repeatedly in the *Daodejing*; in that book, it is never used in quite so explicitly military contexts as in the *Military Methods*, but it does talk about the strength of water residing in its weakness and formlessness. Sunzi and other early military strategists clearly took elements from Daoist non-conflictual ideals and applied them to understanding how military aims could be achieved with the least amount of actual exposure to uncertainty in battle.

The fact that Legalism and military theorists were able to adapt Daoism so easily to the needs of government repression and making war does not mean that Daoism was always a crypto-fascist philosophy. However, it is also not the case that Daoism is really and truly a twenty-first-century philosophy of happy, crunchy Left-coast leftism, and that Han Fei and Sunzi were just nasty men who perverted its true spiritual insights. Early Daoist texts are inherently vague and confusing, the natural result of a philosophical skepticism that language can adequately represent the truth of the world. Some clear themes are voiced again and again throughout the *Daodejing* and the *Zhuangzi*, but these are not books that give very clear instructions as to how their themes should be applied in the real world.

Because these texts are so open to interpretation and appropriation, it is no wonder that they have been used in all kinds of different ways, to support different types of government action and inaction. It is one reason why I felt justified in applying its lessons to protest culture and activism in this book—given that Daoism has been so protean in its historical influence within and beyond China, it seems like more fair game for out-of-context invocation than, say, the very wordy, buttoned-down works of the British Empiricists.

The scope of my own appropriation in this book pales in comparison to the turn that Daoism took at the very end of China's classical period, transforming from an inchoate philosophy into a hierarchical polytheistic religion. And this transformation also radically changed its orientation with respect to worldly power.

A Quick History Lesson: Daoism and Chinese Social Movements

Religion and Rebellion

In the second century AD, the great Han dynasty empire was on its last legs. This dynasty, which played a key role in the consolidation of China's classical culture and political organization, had stumbled into chaos. Rebellions by conquered tributary nations and attacks from other ethnicities on the Han's periphery combined with factional struggles at court to render the government sluggish and ineffective. By the end of the second century, flooding, large-scale population migration, and disease outbreaks had caused a situation of mass popular misery; in that setting of desperation, new forms of religion were able to take hold in China for the first time.

There is good evidence that the early texts of Daoism had some metaphysical elements and may have been in use for certain forms of spiritual practice and belief systems, but in its earliest years it was never a "religion" as we normally understand that word. It had no church, no theology, no set cosmology, no canon of ethics. It deeply influenced the mainstream of Chinese thought, but it may have started from the top down, influencing elites' philosophical assumptions and then slowly moving into popular consciousness.

During the last years of the Han, Daoism suddenly and spectacularly reemerged in the historical record in a new way: as a form of hierarchical religion, with divinities, clergy, full cosmologies and theologies, and social organization of believers into a church structure. The mysterious Dao was reconceived as the supreme deity; Laozi became a deity just slightly below the Dao in the heavenly hierarchy, and Zhuangzi emerged as a major saint. Two versions of religious Daoism appeared almost simultaneously: the "Yellow Turbans" in the northeast and the "Five Pecks of Rice" movement in the southwest. Both rose in rebellion against the Han dynasty.

The Yellow Turban revolt spread quickly around northern China and met with some temporary success, seizing regional control for about a year before the imperial armies put down the main force of the rebellion. For years afterward, however, survivors of the rebellion and other converts across the empire continued to raise smaller regional revolts around the empire. Meanwhile, in Sichuan, the "Five Pecks of Rice" rebellion grew somewhat less rapidly but also was more stable. Built upon a Daoist church movement that had been founded decades earlier, the movement declared itself an independent theocratic state and managed to fend off the imperial army sent against it. Finally defeated by the warlord Cao Cao, the leaders of the movement recognized the new Wei dynasty founded by his son and received, in turn, official freedom to practice and promote their religion. This sect of Daoism that grew out of the Five Pecks of Rice movement, called the "Celestial Masters" or "Orthodox Unity" school, has continued to this day and is the oldest of China's Daoist religious sects.

The way that this trajectory played out, from rebellion against one dynasty to co-optation and endorsement by the next, set the stage for much of imperial China's experience of religion and politics, right up to the modern period. Emperors learned the benefits of winning the ideological support of the Daoist and Buddhist churches, and the latter certainly enjoyed the benefits of state financial support. However, religion is a dangerous thing when it gets loose, and many of China's peasant rebellions over the centuries were affiliated with one or another form of millenarian religion. Belief in an alternative authority structure, greater than that flowing from the emperor, can lead people to kill and to be killed.

Nothing in the texts of ancient Daoism naturally lent itself to becoming the ideology of millenarian peasant rebellions. Not all of those were Daoist—some were Buddhist, and one nineteenth-century one was even a heretical version of Christianity. But the very long distance between the Daoist (and other) religions that spurred these rebellions and the original context of the earliest Daoist texts is instructive. One certainly doesn't need a divinity to lead a revolution: it helps, but other totalizing ideologies can help as well. Belief systems, such as early Daoism, that are both ill-defined and skeptical in orientation don't become the foundation of militancy. Over the length of China's imperial period, the philosophical influence of the early Daoist texts, minus the popular polytheism, remained vibrant among China's intellectual class—but it never drove them into their own palace putsches.

The totalizing beliefs systems of these millenarian movements never succeeded in their aims. China had many emperors who effectively established state religions supported by the monarchy, but there was never a theocratic government brought to power by a successful popular rebellion. The only totalizing ideology that was ever able to bring a popular rebellion to power was, of course, Communism.

Contemporary Daoism and State Control

Because the Chinese Communist Party has understood very well the lessons of Chinese history, and the power of religion to stimulate rebellion, it has placed religion under tight control. Though officially atheist, China also has five state-supported religions: Daoism, Buddhism, Islam, Protestantism, and Catholicism. Long under the direct control of the state, these have recently been moved into the bureaucracy of the Party to guarantee extra-tight ideological control. All legal temples, churches, mosques, monasteries, religious colleges, and any other religious institution is directly under this hierarchy and reports to the party. Adherents are thus provided with a safely patriotic venue for expressing their faith and are, of course, registered and tracked. Any religious organization outside of the state-sanctioned ones is suppressed, sometimes with prison sentences.

A few years ago, I visited a Daoist temple in China that was, like many, both open to the public as a tourist site and a working temple with priests who carried out regular rituals. I happened to get in a discussion with a priest who had been assigned to sell incense to tourists, and he was very eager to talk about international politics and to tell me about the wisdom of the Communist Party. I asked him how he reconciled his position as a Daoist priest with the fact that the Party was officially atheist. He was not bothered by the question at all and answered simply that once the Communist Party was able to lead China to conquer the world, it would then be much easier to make Daoism the universal religion of humanity.

Chinese intellectuals, as a general rule, don't believe in Daoist religion. As the inheritors of various streams of China's classical civilization, most will have at least a passing familiarity with Confucianism and Daoism, though, of course, every individual gives the most thought to issues within his field of specialization. Even those who do know classical thought traditions very well are still living in the twenty-first century, not necessarily taking their cues for how to live from China's ancient wisdom traditions. With that said, in mostly unintentional ways the intellectual class has replicated the impulses to retirement of both Daoism and Confucianism. The state cannot be resisted. It has developed systems of control that can extirpate any organizational nub around which resistance can coalesce. And so, although China has plenty of local wildcat strikes, it has no meaningful intellectuals' resistance. No dissident samizdat journals. No covert underground organizations. Not even marginally liberal class lectures: cameras have now been installed in most lecture halls.

That does not mean that there is thought control or assent. Faculty show up to regular mandatory ideological indoctrination sessions and bring novels to read. Then they go drinking and laugh at the party secretary who wasted two hours claiming the public space of the hall for orthodoxy. Private conversations do not get claimed, and private spaces are not bugged. People say and think what they want—and tend to know exactly what is going on in the outside world, despite a perfect censorship regime and tight control over foreign travel. Topics too sensitive for classrooms are discussed in office hours. In other words, the intellectual labor of thinking the truth, and telling it, goes on. It just has to be carried on in ways that do not confront the state head-on. Intentionally or not, activist-minded work among Chinese scholars and intellectuals takes on the form of Daoist water, flowing away from the heights toward the places of low resistance. This is not the standard form of intellectual heroism, including by the standards of modern Chinese historiography. But I tend to think that real heroes are ones who don't need the pose of heroism.

Further Reading on Daoism and Chinese History

Most of the following should be quite accessible to intelligent general readers without any prior knowledge of China; some are primarily intended for classroom use, but none requires highly technical or scholarly knowledge of Chinese history or culture. For those readers who wish to do a very deep dive on any aspect of traditional China, the place to start is Endymion Wilkinson's *Chinese History: A New Manual*, now in two volumes as of its sixth edition. Wilkinson's book is a reference work that gives the current state of scholarship on a bewildering array of China-centered topics, along with extensive annotated bibliographies of must-read works in Chinese, English, and other languages on each topic.

Stephen Bokenkamp, *Early Daoist Scriptures*. Berkeley: University of California Press, 1997.

> A sourcebook of translated scriptures of explicitly religious Daoist texts, *not* early Daoist philosophical texts such as the *Daodejing* and *Zhuangzi*. One of the few sources available to the general reader that gives a good idea of what Daoist religions believed and practiced through guided readings of their sacred scriptures.

Further Reading on Daoism and Chinese History

Steve Coutinho, *An Introduction to Daoist Philosophies*. New York: Columbia University Press, 2013.

> Intended as an undergraduate-level introduction to Daoist philosophy, this book is divided into sections that treat separately the *Daodejing*, the *Zhuangzi*, and the *Liezi*. A good book for introducing the differing philosophical outlooks of those three early texts.

A. C. Graham, *Disputers of the Tao*. Chicago: Open Court, 1989.

> Graham's survey of early Chinese philosophy is the best English-language introductory survey of the subject for those looking to understand the context in which Daoism emerged. A few of Graham's assertions no longer match scholarly consensus after three decades, but the book as a whole remains an invaluable work by a central figure in the field.

Charles O. Hucker, *China's Imperial Past*. Stanford, CA: Stanford University Press, 1975.

> A classic history of premodern China intended for the general reader and written by one of the preeminent historians of imperial China of his day. For those who do not have the time or interest for all 474 pages, Hucker published an abridged version, *China to 1850*, which is still in print from Stanford.

D. C. Lau, trans., *Tao Te Ching*. New York: Penguin, 1964.

> The *Daodejing* is the fourth-most-translated book of all time. There are many excellent translations, and even more terrible translations, sometimes by people who do not actually know any classical Chinese. Lau's easily available Penguin Classics translation is a model for rendering reasonable readings of the original text into lyrical and accessible English prose and verse.

Hans-Georg Moeller, *Daoism Explained*. Chicago: Open Court, 2004.

    A short book for nonexperts by a leading scholar of philosophical Daoism, introducing the school in historical context and explaining the main ideas of its earliest philosophical works.

Isabelle Robinet, *Taoism: Growth of a Religion*. Translated by Phyllis Brooks. Stanford, CA: Stanford University Press, 1997.

    A classic short introduction to Daoist religions, from the second century AD to the present, by an acclaimed French scholar of religious Daoism.

Brook Ziporyn, trans., *Zhuangzi: The Essential Writings*. Indianapolis: Hackett, 2009.

    An excellent twenty-first-century English translation of Zhuangzi. Ziporyn, an accomplished scholar of Daoism, has managed the difficult task of rendering the original text correctly while preserving the anarchic and puckish humor of the prose.

Acknowledgments

An odd book requires eclectic thanks.

First, and most obviously, I am grateful to my editor, Jonathan Kurtz, who saw the potential in a different kind of book. I hope readers who like this book will repay his gamble by recommending the book to friends.

I'm very grateful to several colleagues who were willing to listen supportively when I needed to talk about the stress I felt from watching activism gone awry, including Valentina Galvani, Tanya Harnett, Christopher Lupke, Aya Fujiwara, Anne Commons, Robert Wood, and Carrie Smith. None of them necessarily agree with my conclusions here, but their willingness to hear about my struggles at a difficult time meant a great deal. At a critical juncture, I needed thorough and compassionate professional care, which I received from my doctor, Alice Bedard, and my therapist, Edmond Okolie. I hope that anyone reading this who is struggling with politically induced depression will be able to find similarly caring professionals.

Many current and former graduate students played important roles, direct or indirect, in helping me move this project forward. Dr. Jenn Quist, who unlike me is an actual writer as well as being an expert on Daoist modes of composition, provided invaluable advice on both an early draft and on the process of finding a publisher. Professor Haiyan Xie of Central China Normal University was very forgiving in allowing me to slack off from my half of a translation project she and I had been working on, without which grace this book wouldn't have moved into production on time. My current advisees have provided the stimulus of their own research discoveries, which continue to push me to think harder about my own arguments—thank you to Belinda Wang, Leyi Zhou, Christian Pak, Madison Coelho, and Chris Wang.

A vast number of Chinese friends, family, colleagues, and long-dead authors have given me constant inspiration—in some cases about the profundities of Chinese civilization, in others more direct wisdom about how to live well in a world one does not control. Any insights in this book were theirs before they were mine.

Although there are many allusions in this book to many sources, one usage in particular requires acknowledgment. To my knowledge, Brook Ziporyn was the first to use the English word "course" as a translation of the Chinese *dao*; this was an excellent choice, and I follow in his footsteps in the second and third sections of this book.

Finally, my family has played a major role here as well: my daughter has frequently been a valuable check on my worst excesses, reminding me of the strong case to be made for carefully delineated distinctions, despite what Zhuangzi might say. And my wife has played the largest role in making this book happen through her daily, unbounded support.

www.ingramcontent.com/pod-product-compliance
Lightning Source LLC
LaVergne TN
LVHW041631060526
838200LV00040B/1537